Success, Your Style!

Right- and Left-Brain Techniques for Learning

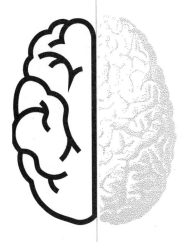

Nancy Lightfoot Matte
Phoenix College and
South Mountain Community College

Susan Hilary Green Henderson
Arizona State University

Wadsworth Publishing Company
I(T)P™ An International Thomson Publishing Company

Belmont • Albany • Bonn • Boston • Cincinnati • Detroit • London • Madrid • Melbourne
Mexico City • New York • Paris • San Francisco • Singapore • Tokyo • Toronto • Washington

Editor: Angela Gantner Wrahtz
Development Editor: Alan Venable
Production Editor: Melanie Field
Designer: John Odam
Print Buyer: Randy Hurst
Permissions Editor: Robert Kauser
Copy Editor: Tom Briggs
Illustrator: Betsy Kopshina and Julie Trei
Cover Designer: Nicole Arigoni
Compositor: Thompson Type, Inc.
Printer: Malloy Lithography, Inc.

This book is printed on
acid-free recycled paper.

Wadsworth Publishing Company
10 Davis Drive
Belmont, California 94002
USA

International Thomson Publishing Europe
Berkshire House 168-173
High Holborn
London, WC1V 7AA
England

Thomas Nelson Australia
102 Dodds Street
South Melbourne 3205
Victoria, Australia

Nelson Canada
1120 Birchmount Road
Scarborough, Ontario
Canada M1K 5G4

International Thomson Editores
Campos Eliseos 385, Piso 7
Col. Polanco
11560 México D.F. México

International Thomson Publishing GmbH
Königswinterer Strasse 418
53227 Bonn
Germany

International Thomson Publishing Asia
221 Henderson Road
#05-10 Henderson Building
Singapore 0315

International Thomson Publishing Japan
Hirakawacho Kyowa Building, 3F
2-2-1 Hirakawacho
Chiyoda-ku, Tokyo 102
Japan

Library of Congress Cataloging-in-Publication Data
Matte, Nancy Lightfoot.
    Success, your style! : right- and left-brain techniques for learning /
Nancy Lightfoot Matte and Susan Hilary Green Henderson.
        p.   cm.
    Includes index.
    ISBN 0-534-24468-8
    1. Study skills.   2. Learning.   3. Left and right (Psychology)
I. Henderson, Susan Hilary Green.   II. Title.
LB2395.M386   1995
378.1′7—dc20
                                          94-41287

*T*o Jim and Ada, who first taught me about education and learning; to Brice and Aly, who are striving for success their way; and to the future grandchild—a current and future success.

—NLM

and

*T*o Erin, Ben, and Abby, who I hope will use this book someday, and to Mark, a constant source of support and strength.

—SGH

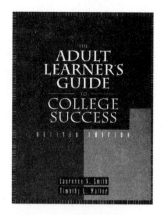

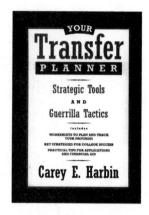

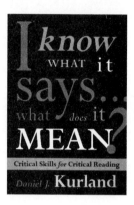

The Wadsworth College Success_sm_ Series

The Adult Learner's Guide to College Success, Revised Edition by Laurence N. Smith and Timothy L. Walter, ISBN: 0-534-23298-1

Learning Your Way Through College by Robert N. Leamnson, ISBN: 0-534-24504-8

Your Transfer Planner: Strategic Tools and Guerrilla Tactics by Carey E. Harbin, ISBN: 0-534-24372-X

I Know What It Says . . . What Does It Mean?: Critical Skills for Critical Reading by Daniel J. Kurland, ISBN: 0-534-24486-6

Mastering Mathematics: How to Be a Great Math Student, Second Edition by Richard Manning Smith, ISBN: 0-534-20838-X

Right from the Start: Managing Your Way to College Success by Robert Holkeboer, ISBN: 0-534-19290-4

Turning Point by Joyce D. Weinsheimer, ISBN: 0-534-19422-2

The Language of Learning: Vocabulary for College Success, Second edition by Jane N. Hopper and Jo Ann Carter-Wells, ISBN: 0-534-21384-7

Merlin: The Sorcerer's Guide to College Success by Christopher F. Monte, ISBN: 0-534-13482-3

The Freshman Year Experience_sm_ Series

Your College Experience: Strategies for Success, Second Edition by John N. Gardner and A. Jerome Jewler, ISBN: 0-534-30960-7

Your College Experience: Strategies for Success, Concise Edition by A. Jerome Jewler and John N. Gardner, ISBN: 0-534-19962-3

College Is Only the Beginning: A Student Guide to Higher Education, Second Edition by John N. Gardner and A. Jerome Jewler, ISBN: 0-534-09642-5

Create Your College Success: Activities and Exercises for Students by Robert A. Friday, ISBN: 0-534-09318-3

Step by Step to College Success by A. Jerome Jewler and John N. Gardner, ISBN: 0-534-07998-9

The Senior Year Experience_sm_ Series

Ready for the Real World by William C. Hartel, Stephen W. Schwartz, Steven D. Blume, and John N. Gardner, ISBN: 0-534-17712-3

For more information or to purchase any of these Wadsworth texts, please contact your campus store.

Contents

Chapter 6   Reading College Textbooks   86

Chapter 7   Using Memorization Techniques   106

Chapter 8   Studying for Tests   120

Chapter 9   Taking Objective Tests   136

Chapter 10   Writing Essay Exams   164

Epilogue: What Next?   177

Appendix A   Writing Assignments   179

Preface

We have been teachers of college students in various settings for a combined 35 years and have learned much from them. Many of our students came to our institutions believing that they lacked the tools necessary to succeed. As we worked with them, however, they discovered, in their struggle *to learn how to learn,* how capable and bright they really are.

As we learned to help each student discover his or her strengths and abilities, we came to understand how differently each of us processes and produces information. From this understanding, we developed our classes and syllabi. What started as a compilation of notes, thoughts, and ideas has culminated in this book.

Success, Your Style! is written for today's college student: young and old, of many races and backgrounds, and with varying levels of preparation for higher education. The material is divided into ten chapters. Chapter 1, "Starting Smart: The First Few Weeks," will help you prepare for the first hectic weeks of school. Chapter 2, "Assessing Your Learning Style," will provide you the foundation needed to access your brain dominance and utilize many of the tips in the book. Chapter 3, "Managing Your Time," explains how you can organize your time—a key to college success. Chapter 4, "Recognizing Discipline Information Patterns," will help you customize your learning style to specific disciplines such as art history, foreign languages, history, literature, math, and science. Chapters 5 and 6, "Taking Lecture Notes" and "Reading College Text-books," will present systems for taking in-class and reading notes. Chapter 7, "Using Memorization Techniques," gives you tools to help you retain material. Chapters 8, 9, and 10— "Studying for Tests," "Taking Objective Tests," and "Writing Essay Exams"—focus on test preparation and test taking. In addition, Appendix A, "Writing Assignments," gives you a framework for researching, organizing, and composing various types of writing assignments. Appendix B, "College Services and Procedures," outlines the wide variety of available services at your school and ways to access them.

This book is written the same way we teach: from a whole-brain learning styles approach. Each chapter begins with a "TIPS" section, followed by a left-brained and right-brained overview of key points. Each chapter includes exercises for both right- and left-brained learners. And each chapter contains a summary of the main points and links current material to what follows.

An extensive *Instructors Resource Manual* is available to adopters. This detailed text contains sample lesson plans, class activities, class lectures, test questions, and exercises and cooperative learning tips for each chapter. In addition, the *Instructors Resource Manual* contains a "Syllabus Evaluation Worksheet" to help instructors plan their syllabi as well as important background information.

We welcome any feedback you might have about this text and encourage you to contact us if you have questions or ideas for us.

Acknowledgments

Deep and heartfelt thanks go to all those who have helped this book project come to fruition.

We wish to thank the administrations of Arizona State University, South Mountain Community College, and Phoenix College for their support. Gary Krahenbuhl, Sam Kirkpatrick, Christine Wilkinson, Lynne Bensted, and Brice Corder stood by this program during many lean years and deserve special thanks.

Many thanks to the following reviewers for their comments: Rose Baugh, Georgia College; Rennie W. Brantz, Appalachian State University; Joseph W. Capers, Grambling State University; James Cebulski, University of South Florida; Joanne E. Fowler, Kennesaw State College; Pete Gustafson, Rose-Hulman Institute of Technology; Lawrence C. Henson, Weber State University; Pam Hill, Palo Alto College; Sall Kirst, University of Arkansas at Monticello; Rebecca Leonard, North Carolina State University; Carole Obermeyer, Newberry College; Kathy Shipley, California State University, Stanislaus; and Greg Smith, University of Wisconsin, Rock County.

The faculty and staffs of South Mountain College and the UNI and LIA 100 programs at Arizona State University contributed much to this project. Of particular help were Mary Ellen Reed, Sallee Clements, Chris Lash, Lois Roma-Deeley, Brian Richardson, Marilyn Enloe, Isobel LeRoy, Debbie Anderson, Betty Elliott, and Kate Lynch-Randall.

Thanks also to Bob and Lila Green for the encouragement they gave; to Carol, Janet, and Bert Green for the support to keep going; and to Dan Green, who first showed Sue it was possible to learn successfully, differently. Special thanks to John Gardner and USC staff for encouragement and support over the years.

And to the thousands of students who have shared their struggles and successes with us, this book could never have been written without you and your valuable input. Thank you!

Nancy L. Matte, Ph.D.
Professor of English and
* Composition*
1202 W. Thomas
Phoenix College
Phoenix, Arizona 85013
Matte @ PC.maricopa.edu

Sue Henderson, M.S.
Associate Director, Undergraduate
* Academic Services*
Director, University 100 Program
Arizona State University
Tempe, Arizona 85287-3801
ICSHH @ ASUVM.INRE.ASU.EDU

Your guide to learning with
Success, Your Style!

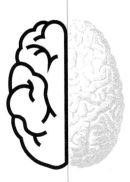

IF YOU'VE EVER SAILED THROUGH one class and struggled through another, you have an idea that no two learning situations, and no two learners, are the same. *Success, Your Style!* is designed to help you discover the ways in which you learn most naturally, and to show you how to enhance your performance in any course based on that knowledge.

In its approach and in its visual design, *Success Your Style!* is set up to help you determine the traits that make up your personal learning style. Armed with this self-knowledge, you can make more informed decisions about which study strategies work best for you. You'll also learn how you can adapt your style for better results in different types of courses. To get the most out of this discovery process, take a few moments to familiarize yourself with the tools and techniques you'll use along the way.

Your Personal Learning Style Summary

A key to forming a clear picture of your learning style is the Personal Learning Style Summary in Chapter Two. By working through the summary you'll build a much better sense of how you organize and process information, and how you turn it into knowledge. Once you complete the summary, you can use it to determine which study strategies to make your own.

PERSONAL LEARNING STYLE SUMMARY

Take some of the assessments on learning styles discussed in the Prologue and in this chapter. Record the results here and use it to help identify the most effective study place, time, and environment for yourself. Note that as you learn more approaches to studying, your habits and preferences may change. Thus you may find it interesting to answer these questions again at the end of the quarter, semester, or year.

1. I am a(n) _____ visual _____ auditory _____ kinesthetic processor.
2. My score on items 1–5 of the informal learning style assessment was _____ .
3. I tend to be a _____ left-brained _____ combination _____ right-brained person.
4. My score on items 6–15 of the informal learning style assessment was _____ .
5. My score on the informal speaking style assessment was _____ , making me _____ .
6. My score on the formal speaking style assessment was _____ , making me _____ .
7. My score on the listening style assessment was _____ , making me _____ .
8. My scores on any other learning style assessments I've taken:
   a. MBTI _____
   b. Kolb _____
   c. LASSI _____
   d. Other _____
9. I am most intellectually alert in the (*circle one*) (a) early morning, (b) mid-morning, (c) early afternoon, (d) late afternoon, (e) early evening, (f) late evening, (g) midnight-to-dawn hours. This is your Prime Internal Time. (*Tip*: Schedule some of your intellectually challenging reading or study during a portion of your Prime Internal Time.)
10. I am least intellectually alert in the (*circle one*) (a) early morning, (b) mid-morning, (c) early afternoon, (d) late afternoon, (e) early evening, (f) late evening, (g) midnight-to-dawn hours. This is your Prime External Time. (*Tip*: Schedule some routine or non-intellectually demanding academic work during a portion of your Prime External Time.)
11. The best place for me to study at home is _____
12. The best place for me to study on campus is _____

27

PERSONAL LEARNING STYLE SUMMARY

Opportunities to try different strategies

Success, Your Style! offers you several different strategies for each study skill. Throughout the book, you'll have the chance to try out a variety of them rather than struggling to use "one-size-fits-all" study techniques. Take the time to sample different techniques and you'll end up with a custom-fit approach to better academic performance.

Time circles Using the time circle shown in Figure 3.1, keep track of how you spend your time each day for four days. Stop once in the morning, once in the afternoon, and once before bed, and color in the appropriate circle hours for each activity. This time circle is much more effective when you use different colors to show various activities. Do *not* fill this chart out in advance. Note, too, that this will not yield a schedule to follow; rather, it will simply give you a realistic picture of where your time is currently going.

At the end of each day, evaluate your use of time. Add up the hours spent on each activity. Make notes or code specific sections to indicate areas where you think you are spending too little time, too much time, and about the right amount of time. When, where, and how did you waste time this day? How do you want tomorrow to differ?

Time logs Using the time log shown in Figure 3.2, keep track of how you spend your time each day for four days. Stop at each mealtime and before bed, and fill out the chart. This time log will help you see where the time has been spent. Do *not* fill this out in advance. Again, this will not result in a schedule to follow, but rather give you a realistic picture of

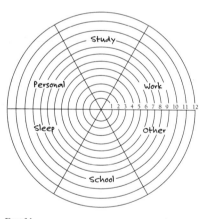

Figure 3.1
Time Circle

EXERCISE 5.1

ATTENDING TO NONVERBAL COMMUNICATION

Pay close attention to one of your instructors. Notice what typical nonverbals she or he uses to emphasize important lecture points. Then, try to discover one or two of her or his individual nonverbals that signal, "This is important." Make sure you take notes on all information signaled by the nonverbal behaviors. You may want to code it so you'll remember that it was stressed nonverbally. This information will guide you in later study so you concentrate on points the instructor considers important.

- Making eye contact with the students
- Lowering the tone of the voice
- Speaking slower and enunciating words more carefully
- Glancing at notes to make sure he or she has the information correct
- Making some physical gesture to emphasize a point
- Writing on the chalkboard or using an overhead projector
- Distributing information on handouts

Spoken information accompanied by these behaviors usually means that the instructor is signaling important information. Code this information in your lecture notes because there's a good chance it'll be a test question.

GENERAL NOTE-TAKING GUIDELINES

Why Take Notes?

Active note-taking is a powerful way to begin learning new material. It turns a passive learning environment into a participatory one. Taking clear, detailed, and organized lecture notes is an excellent way to "study," to save precious time using classtime both to record new information and to begin learning it, and to create thorough, well-organized materials for future study. Moreover, it gives strong clues to potential test questions.

What and How Much Should You Write Down?

At the beginning of the semester, answer these questions for yourself in order to plan your note-taking strategy in each class:

- How much of the lecture information is repeated in the textbook?

Application exercises

Application exercises give you the chance to do just that—apply concepts, tips and techniques to your own life and learning. Included in each chapter of the book, application exercises give you hands-on experience and real-life insights into your optimum learning process. Many of these exercises involve working in pairs or groups with your classmates as you do in many college courses.

Chapter overviews for left- and right-brain learners

Turn to the beginning of any chapter in this book and you will see two kinds of chapter overviews. Why two? One is geared for left-brain dominant learners and the other for right-brain dominant learners. Whichever one you prefer, make sure you study the overview before beginning the chapter. Doing so will give you an idea of what to expect and will help reinforce the concepts and techniques within the chapter. Comparing the two different overviews will also enhance your whole-brain learning.

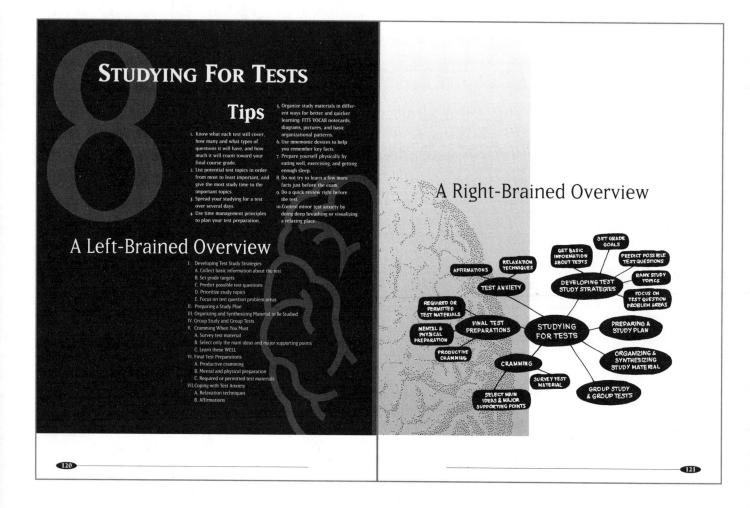

Tips

Also located at the beginning of each chapter are a series of "Tips." These at-a-glance tips give you a quick idea of some of the most important ideas from the following chapter to apply now to your own study habits. Scanning the Tips will help you anticipate the chapter material ahead and you can use the Tips as a quick reference as you study for other classes.

Is This You?

Through the book you'll see a number of special sections that ask "Is This You?" Each "Is This You?" section describes some of the experiences and challenges that may be facing you as a college student and connects those issues to possible solutions within the chapter. Stop for a moment and ask yourself "Is This <u>Me</u>?" Doing so will help you understand how you can address your own particular situation using techniques you select from the book.

You're looking over your notes from one of your lecture courses, and you realize you're in trouble. You tried to write down everything your instructor said, but now all you have is several pages of alien scribble. In this chapter we'll give you a system for taking comprehensive—and comprehensible—notes in your lecture courses. In fact, we'll give you two systems, one left-brained and one right-brained, so that you can adapt a system that works best for you in all your courses.

CLUES TO YOUR INSTRUCTOR'S EXPECTATIONS AND COMMUNICATION STYLE

Before you can take effective lecture notes, you need to understand your instructor's expectations and communication style. This means paying close attention to his or her comments about what the class will cover, what assignments you'll have, how the course grade will be calculated, and what policies govern late papers. It also means attending to the instructor's nonverbal communication behaviors such as physical gestures and facial expressions. Paying attention to a lecturer's nonverbals is a good way to get a sense of what that person is like as well as what he or she thinks is important. Look for these common nonverbal communication behaviors:

CHAPTER 5 TAKING LECTURE NOTES

Part I: Using Bibliographic and Library Tools

Goal of Part I These items are designed to teach you about the research process, to show you how to use various library tools, and to give you information about your college library.

The research process At the beginning of the research process, in one or two work sessions, compile four times the number of final sources you expect to use in your paper. This is not as difficult as it sounds if you use the shortcuts to potential reference sources as outlined in this library project. In actual research you would probably need to locate only one or two of these, but for this project familiarize yourself with all these reference sources:

- Encyclopedias, including any online encyclopedias your college library has in its computer system
- Books that contain only sources—called bibliographies—or books that contain bibliographies
- Bibliographic indexes
- Library guides to a specific subject, if your library provides these

*1. Define a bibliography.

_____

*2. Define a bibliography as used in a research paper.

_____

*3. Define a working bibliography as used in the preparation of a research paper.

_____

_____

Reference stacks Some libraries place often-used reference books together. Check to see if your library does this. If so, complete this section.

4. While browsing in the reference stacks, select a book whose title surprises you (you are surprised to find that such a book was published) but that you think contains useful information:
   Title _____ Call # _____
5. While browsing in the reference stacks, select any book that you would like to write or be referenced in someday:
   Title _____ Call # _____

Almanacs Almanacs are very helpful for locating a number of facts quickly.

Quick References

The appendices at the back of this book give you "at a glance" information on other tasks and procedures you're likely to encounter as a college student. Appendix A includes valuable tips on the form and process of many college writing assignments. Appendix B will help you keep on top of services and procedures that can be critical to your college success.

Prologue:
What Now?

learn *vt* to gain knowledge or understanding of or a skill in by study, instruction, or experience

Webster's Ninth New Collegiate Dictionary

Left brain. Right brain. Visual learner. Auditory processor. Kinesthetic comprehender. Intuitive. Sensor. Haptic. Print. Aural. Interactive. Olfactory. Emotional. Social. Receptive. Expressive. High structure. Low structure. Vertical. Lateral. Abstract conceptualizer. Assimilator. Accommodator. Reflective observer. Active experimenter. Extrovert. Introvert. Thinker. Feeler. Terms and definitions fly around. Your brain feels like mush. No, it doesn't feel like mush! It is mush.

The terms in the first paragraph are only a few of the many used by scientists, researchers, and educators to describe how the human brain learns and how human beings process information. The human brain is a complex and efficient learning organ, and emerging theories about how the human brain works suggest that our brains function on many different levels and in a variety of ways.

In the 1960s Roger Sperry, Michael Gazzaniga, and Jerre Levy did groundbreaking experiments in split-brain research pinpointing the left- and right-brain locations of many mental and physical functions.[1] Howard Gardner in *Frames of Mind* theorizes that there are five intelligences—linguistic, musical, logical-mathematical, spatial, and bodily-kinesthetic. A person may function better in one category than another. David Kolb has developed an inventory that categorizes learners and information processors based on how they process information and what types of learning environments they prefer.[2] Psychologists John Grinder and Richard Bandler developed the neurolinguistic

(NLP) model that describes how individuals use a visual, an auditory, or a kinesthetic method to process sensory information. What all of these experts are attempting to describe is how people make sense of data and learn.

In this book we concentrate on five learning patterns or methods of comprehending information—left- and right-brained, visual, auditory, and kinesthetic—and present learning skills and techniques that use one or more of these patterns. These techniques and strategies have evolved from methods that we've taught to hundreds of our students and that we have found to work. *No one person can use or is expected to use all the techniques and methods we will present in this book.* Experiment with them. Find the ones that work best for you. Adapt and modify them to make them work even better. You are beginning your journey to becoming an independent learner. Bon voyage!

LEARNING PATTERNS

Not everyone learns the same way. More importantly, there is no single right way to learn. Sometime, probably very early in your life, you discovered a way to collect and process information that worked for and made sense to you. You continued using this process, developing and strengthening it until it became your preferred or dominant learning pattern. You use other learning patterns as well as your preferred style, but not as often nor with as much ease. Just as you developed your preferred learning pattern, you can develop other patterns by using and practicing them in order to improve your ability to organize a task or to learn.

Visual, Auditory, or Kinesthetic

You experience the world through your five senses. As your senses collect information, you may begin to organize it by visual, auditory, or kinesthetic means and make sense of it in either a left- or right-brained way. Thus, for example, you may be a right-brained visual or a left-brained auditory processor. Admittedly such classifications oversimplify what the brain actually does. Our purpose is to make you aware of the mental thinking and processing habits you have developed over the years, to show you how you can apply those habits to your academic work, and to suggest ways for you to learn other, useful patterns. But what precisely do we mean when we refer to the various learning patterns?

Visual processors include about 55 percent of the population. These people tend to be fast thinkers, to gesture freely while talking, and to communicate very clearly and concisely. They often use visual description when communicating. Typical phrases of visual processors include "I see," "Picture that," "See

IDENTIFYING YOUR LEARNING PATTERN

A quick and easy way to assess whether someone is a visual, auditory, or kinesthetic processor is to watch that person's eye movements as he or she is describing something that exists in the physical world. Pair up with a friend and take turns doing the following: One of you describe a favorite place or a person you know to the other while that person watches your eye movements. If the speaker's eyes move very distinctively upward and typically to the left, then that person tends to process visually. If there is little or no eye movement, but a fairly steady, straight-ahead gaze, then that person tends to process auditorily. If the speaker glances downward, then that person tends to process kinesthetically.

the light," and "It's clear to me." They find charts, pictures, and diagrams to be good ways to learn, understand, and remember information and concepts.

Auditory processors make up less than 20 percent of the population. These people are sensitive to and often easily distracted by sounds. In conversation, they usually are good listeners but may be slow to answer the other person. They respond positively to smooth, nonmanipulative presentations, while monotonous tones of voice turn them off. Typical phrases of auditory processors include "Tell me," "Can we talk?" "It's clear as a bell," and "That rings true." They find lectures, discussions, and group study to be good ways to learn, understand, and remember information and concepts.

Kinesthetic processors comprise approximately 25 percent of the population. These people are feeling and touch oriented, good at hands-on tasks, good linguists, and very sensitive to others' feelings. They may focus on emotions rather than logic and reason. Typical phrases of kinesthetic processors include "I have a gut feeling," "I am sensing you're right," and "I am getting a handle on it." They find doing hands-on projects or experiments, writing down the information, and applying it to real-life situations to be good ways to learn, understand, and remember information and concepts.[3]

Left- or Right-Brained

Left-brained individuals are analytical, taking things and ideas apart to comprehend something, while right-brained people are holistic, looking for patterns and relationships. Left-brained individuals respond to facts while right-brained people respond to feelings. Left-brained individuals think concretely and rationally while right-brained people think abstractly and

Left-Brained	**Right-Brained**
Responds to facts	Responds to feelings
Has a sense of time and keeps track of time	Has little sense of clock time; relates to things in present time
Has a sense of order or chronology	Has a sense of space and understands spatial relationships
Figures things out with linear, concrete, step-by-step thinking	Figures things out holistically through abstract thinking
Writes	Draws or sketches
Reads music	Recognizes and remembers melodies and musical chords
Uses analytical thinking in which the conclusion comes after the facts	Uses parallel thinking in which the conclusion comes before or with the facts
Uses names to describe and define things	Uses metaphors to describe and define things
Responds to lists	Responds to visuals and colors
Understands language, including grammar, syntax, and word meanings	Understands idiomatic language which requires language pattern to understand
Uses speech and processes words	Processes pictures; draws
Understands language/verbal communication	Understands nonverbals behaviors and emotions
Listens, talks, recites	Expresses emotions, moves, feels
Is more cerebral	Is more physical
Analyzes; looks at parts of the whole	Seeks patterns; takes pieces and puts into a whole or a pattern
Thinks rationally based on facts and reasons and logic	Thinks intuitively based on hunches, feelings, and emotions

Figure P.1
Typical characteristics of Left- and Right-Brained Individuals[4]

intuitively. Figure P.1 lists typical characteristics of left- and right-brained individuals. Review the list to get a sense of whether you tend to lean more to the right or left; and thus of how you perform learning tasks. Chapter 2, "Assessing Your Learning Style," provides several exercises and assessments to help you determine your preferred learning process. You may find it helpful to do some of these early in the semester to get specific ideas about more effective ways to organize academic learning tasks. We recommend especially that you complete the Personal Learning Style Summary in Chapter 2 so that you can begin immediately to learn more efficient ways to study.

Notes

[1]Thomas R. Blakeslee, *The Right Brain: A New Understanding of the Unconscious Mind and Its Creative Powers* (New York: Berkeley Books, 1983).

[2]David Kolb, *Experiential Learning: Experience as the Source of Learning and Development* (Englewood Cliffs, NJ: Prentice-Hall, 1984).

[3]Descriptions of visual, auditory, and kinesthetic processing are based on NLP theory summarized from Michael Brook's *Instant Rapport* (New York: Warner Books, 1989).

[4]Information on right- and left-brain characteristics based on Betty Edwards, *Drawing on the Right Side of the Brain* (Los Angeles: Tarcher, 1979); David Kolb, *Experiential Learning: Experience as the Source of Learning and Development* (Englewood Cliffs, NJ: Prentice-Hall, 1984); and Jacquelyn Wonder and Priscilla Donovan, *Whole Brain Thinking* (New York: Ballantine Books, 1984).

STARTING SMART:
The First Few Weeks

Tips

1. Take care of college paperwork.
2. Get comfortable with your new environment.
3. Start time planning early.
4. Get off to a fast start studying.
5. Survey your textbooks.

A Left-Brained Overview

I. Taking Care of College Paperwork
   A. Register for classes—take care of drop/add if necessary
   B. Pay fees
   C. Establish a record-keeping system
   D. Take care of parking
II. Getting Comfortable with Your New Environment
   A. Get settled in living place
   B. Establish a place to study
   C. Find out where classes meet
   D. Figure out what to wear
   E. Explore available campus resources
III. Early Time Planning
   A. Academic analysis
   B. Your master schedule
IV. Getting Off to a Fast Start Studying
   A. Purchase required textbooks
   B. Save receipts
   C. Survey the books

A Right-Brained Overview

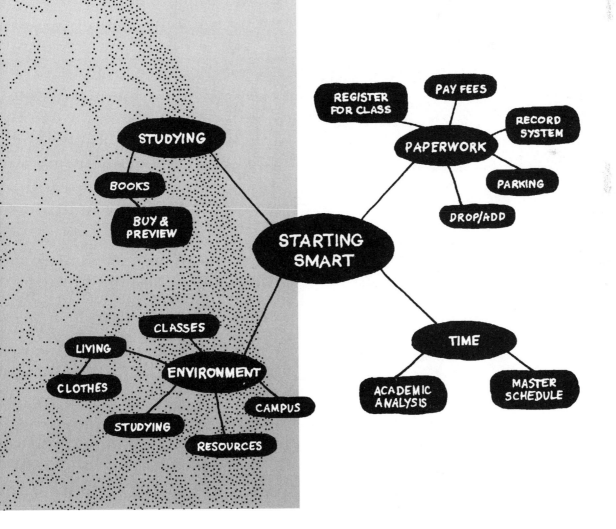

You're new to college and it seems like a whole alien world. You're not sure where to park or where your classes are or even what all the buildings are. And you're worried about making new friends and succeeding academically. In this chapter we'll show you how to get settled in: how to take care of college paperwork, plan your schedule, get comfortable in your new environment, and get off to a good start with your schoolwork.

IS THIS YOU?

TAKING CARE OF COLLEGE PAPERWORK

Your first task is taking care of college paperwork. This means dealing with four basic areas: (1) registration, (2) fees, (3) records and receipts, and (4) parking.

1. Registering for Classes

It's crucial that you find out if you have the proper signatures to register, if you need to take any placement exams, and if there are any prerequisites for the classes you hope to take. (At some colleges it is possible to preregister or register early for classes the semester prior to enrollment and/or over the phone. Find out if this is available at your school—and if so, use it.)

Most colleges have a period of time when you can drop and/or add classes without fees or penalties. At many schools this is a short period of time—often only a few days long. No matter how busy you are, get a printout of your official schedule from your college registrar during the first week of school. First, check it for accuracy. It is possible that you could be enrolled in a class and not even know it. Then, early on, make a decision about your schedule. Are there any classes you want to drop? If so, will you add another in its place? Make sure you keep enough credit hours to be eligible for financial aid, scholarships, and insurance. If you are going to drop/add, be sure to do it officially. *Never* just quit going to class and assume that you will be dropped from the roster. Make sure the drop is official or you could end up with a failing grade in a class you never even attended.

2. Paying Fees

At some colleges, if your fees are not paid by a certain date your registration is invalidated. If you are receiving financial aid, have a scholarship, or are having your fees waived for any reason, you still have to let the cashier or fee payment office know. Don't assume that your coach, counselor, or financial aid officer is taking care of this for you. Check to see that your fees are paid and applied to your bill.

3. Keeping Receipts and Records

It's a good idea to establish a file, a shoebox, a notebook—someplace—where you keep your school records. Important documents include transcripts, receipts for fee payments, records of dropping or adding classes, notes about classes to take or avoid, and lists of classes required for graduation. Don't expect the school or others to do this for you. Even if you have an advisor who keeps some of these records, make copies for yourself. Since having these documents is ultimately *your* responsibility and not your counselor's, protect yourself.

4. Taking Care of Parking

If you are planning on driving to school, you will need to get a parking permit. Find out where and when you can park on your campus. Many schools give out tickets during the first weeks of classes, so be sure you are parking legally. (If you get a parking ticket, pay it. At many colleges your grades will be withheld or you will be barred from getting future registration if you have outstanding parking fines.) If you are attending a school with normally crowded parking, assume that the parking problem will be at its worst during the first few weeks of classes and plan accordingly. Come to school extra early on the first days, and have a backup parking plan in case your first plan doesn't pan out.

CHECKING YOUR PAPERWORK

For each of the following questions, circle the appropriate response. For each "no" response, make plans to resolve the situation.

1. Have you registered for classes?   yes   no
2. Have you checked your schedule for accuracy?   yes   no
3. Have you officially dropped/added courses?   yes   no
4. Have you paid your fees?   yes   no
5. Have you established a record-keeping system?   yes   no
6. Have you taken care of parking?   yes   no

GETTING COMFORTABLE WITH YOUR NEW ENVIRONMENT

It's important to become as comfortable as possible with your new environment. This means dealing with six basic issues: (1) your living place, (2) a study area, (3) class locations, (4) clothing, (5) campus resources, and (6) meals.

1. Settling into Your Living Place

If you are moving to live near or on campus, get moved in at least a week *before* school begins. You'll have plenty to do during the first week of school, and you don't need the added pressure of organizing your living space during that time.

If you will be sharing a place with a new roommate or roommates, spend time both getting acquainted and establishing rules for living together. Getting to know and learning how to get along with new and different people is one nonacademic advantage of college life. You don't have to become best buddies with your roommate. It does help, however, if you are on speaking terms. If you start to experience problems or tensions in this area, deal with it sooner rather than later. Visit your college's counseling or residence life center for help as soon as problems arise.

If you are living away from home, especially for the first time, you will need time to "build your nest." This involves giving your living place some of your own personality and defining that space as your own. Bring some favorite treasures with you, or buy some posters or plants that reflect your personality. If you have roommates, define some space that is solely yours. Having a nest to which you can retreat will help reduce the feeling of impersonality you may experience in new places.

If you are living at home, you may want to establish a new study space that signifies the start of this new chapter in your life. This could be a desk area, a den, or a shelf where you keep your school materials. Be sure your family, children, spouse, parents, roommates, and even pets respect this space.

2. Establishing a Place to Study

One of the keys to succeeding in college is to have an appropriate environment for study. Many students find it is helpful to establish a place for study and to study there regularly. Stock this place with the tools you will need: a dictionary and thesaurus, pencils and pens, staplers, and the like. Check that your study area is well lit, has a comfortable chair, and is neither too warm nor too cold.

3. Finding Out Where Your Classes Meet

The first step is to get a campus map *before* the first day of school. Spend an hour or so walking around campus and locating all your class buildings and marking them on the map. If possible, go into the buildings and find the classrooms. Practice following your daily schedule, walking from building to building as you will on your first day of classes. Note where there are restrooms along the way.

4. Figuring Out What to Wear

No, most American colleges do not currently have dress codes set by the administration. However, at many schools there is an "accepted dress norm" for many students. At some Arizona colleges students wear shorts to school for twelve months; at some East Coast schools the dress is often more formal than at some western schools where jeans are the norm. As you wander about campus, note how others are dressed. What is the prevailing norm? Do you want to dress similarly or differently? There is not one right way to dress, and since you may not be able to get a totally accurate picture during the first week, you may want to hold off buying new clothes until after school begins. Then you can decide about what to buy, what to keep, and what to discard.

5. Checking Out Campus Resources

Most colleges have many resources available to students ranging from child care centers to gymnasiums, from bicycle repair co-ops to counseling centers. Find out what resources are available at your school and where they are located. If you think you will want tutoring in any of your classes, sign up early! For a more complete checklist of campus resources, see Appendix B.

6. Figuring Out Where to Eat

Commuter students and residential students alike will often be on campus at mealtime. Figure out where you will eat or

CHECKING YOUR ENVIRONMENT

For each of the following questions, circle the appropriate response. For each "no" response, make plans to resolve the situation.

1. Have you gotten settled in your living place?   yes   no
2. Have you established a place to study?   yes   no
3. Have you found out where your classes will meet?   yes   no
4. Have you figured out what to wear?   yes   no
5. Have you checked out available campus resources?   yes   no
6. Have you registered for tutoring?   yes   no
7. Have you figured out where to eat?   yes   no

purchase food. Is there a prepaid meal plan available? If so, is it for residential students or all students? Is there a place where you can store food brought from home or heat it up? Especially during the first few weeks of school, most campus dining establishments are crowded. You may want to pack a few snacks until you find a place where you can eat in a timely and affordable manner.

EARLY TIME PLANNING

Once you arrive on campus and register for classes, it may seem that everything happens at a hectic pace. It is normal to feel rushed when you are unfamiliar with your surroundings. Time management is a vital tool for college success and is discussed in depth in Chapter 3. However, some time management tools should be used starting the first day and week of classes—specifically, those related to academic analysis and to a master schedule.

Academic Analysis

In order to succeed in college, you need to have an overall sense of the classes you will be taking. To do this, it is vital to attend all classes starting with the very first one. Many students think that not much will be covered during that first class— but they are *wrong*! Students can gather a first impression of the class and instructor during the early classes that will invaluable as the semester progresses. During the first day of class you should do the following:

1. **Find out your instructors' names**.
2. **Get a syllabus for each class**. This syllabus should contain information about what the class will cover, what books will be used, what types of examinations or

ANALYZING YOUR ACADEMIC LIFE

Fill in the chart shown in Figure 1.1 with pertinent information from all your classes.

evaluations will be given, and when and where the instructor plans to hold office hours (times when a student can meet with an instructor in his or her office to discuss matters relevant to the class). You will learn about homework assignments, extra credit options, reading lists, and so forth. If you are not given this information, ask for it.

3. **Get to know your classmates**. From the first day you will be able to sense if the class is a large, lecture-type course or a smaller, discussion-type seminar. Introduce yourself to at least one person in each of your classes. Exchange names and phone numbers. Agree to back each other up if one of you is absent during class. Address your new classmate by name before leaving, and state that you look forward to seeing her or him at your next class meeting.

Your Master Schedule

Although your schedule will certainly change as the semester progresses, it is important that you rough out an idea of what your early weeks of school will be like. You can complete this master schedule as soon as you register, prior to the start of classes. This first schedule should, at the very least, indicate the following:

- Your classes
- Your work schedule
- Any regular weekly activity such as athletic practice, club meetings, and so on
- Times for social life, recreation, and personal care
- Time to study for each class

STARTING YOUR MASTER SCHEDULE

Fill out the schedule shown in Figure 1.2 for your first week of classes using the guidelines noted above.

At first you probably won't have a clear idea of how much you should study for each class. That is OK! But, in order not to fall behind, choose a regular time to study for each class. During the first week of school, follow your plan but note what works and doesn't work. This will give you an idea of how to alter your schedule so it is more workable in the coming weeks.

GETTING OFF TO A FAST START STUDYING

Starting any new task can be the hardest part of finishing it. This is certainly true for starting to study your class materials. It is very hard to know where to begin and what to do first. Here are some tips to get you off to a fast start studying.

CLASSES					
Instructor name					
Office location					
Office hours					
Phone number					
Class type (lecture, discussion, seminar, laboratory)					
Texts required					
Texts recommended					
Required materials					
Grading system					
Exams: number and type					
Value of exams					
Other grade sources					
Extra credit sources (if any)					
Attendance policies and penalties					
Late-paper policies and penalties					
Make-up policy					
Written work format					
Instructor's likes/dislikes					
Instructor's body language					
Grade goals (maximum/minimum)					
Study hours needed weekly (estimate)					

Figure 1.1
Academic Analysis and Goals

CHAPTER 1   STARTING SMART: THE FIRST FEW WEEKS

A.M. 6–7	Sunday	Monday	Tuesday	Wednesday	Thursday	Friday	Saturday
7–8							
8–9							
9–10							
10–11							
11–12							
P.M. 12–1							
1–2							
2–3							
3–4							
4–5							
5–6							
6–7							
7–8							
8–9							
9–10							
10–11							
11–12							
A.M. 12–1							
1–2							

Figure 1.2
Your Master Schedule

PREPARING TO SUCCEED ACADEMICALLY

For each of the following questions, circle the appropriate response. For each "no" response, make plans to resolve the situation.

1. Have you purchased all the required texts for all your classes?   yes   no

2. Did you save your receipts?   yes   no

3. Have you spent about 30 minutes previewing each text?   yes   no

4. Have you evaluated your class schedule to determine if you can handle each course's requirements and achieve your course grade goals? Have you officially dropped and added if necessary?   yes   no

First, if possible, purchase your required textbooks *before* classes start. Most campus bookstores have lists of the required texts for each class. However, hold off buying any book labeled "optional" or "supplementary" until after you have consulted with your instructor. Often the optional texts are used very rarely and are also available in the college library.

Once you purchase the required texts, *be sure to save your receipts*! Occasionally instructors will change their minds at the last minute and decide to use a different text. If you save your receipts, you'll be able to get a full refund or exchange.

Next, after you bring your books home, look through them—even before you are assigned to do so. This will give you a good head start in understanding the material being presented in the class. Begin by reading the preface or introduction to find out why and to whom the author wrote the book. Scan the table of contents; often the table of contents is really an outline of the entire book. Try to figure out how the book is set up. Are there introductory paragraphs or lists of important ideas at the beginning of each chapter? Does each chapter have a summary?

Frequently the first day of a college class is like any other class session. After distributing the syllabus, the instructor begins teaching the material. You may even have homework on the very first night of school. It is tempting to wait to study until the weekend, or closer to test time, but this is where many students fall behind and never catch up. Begin your assigned reading the very first night, and work ahead if you have a chance. Work all problems in your math texts, complete all the assigned science exercises, and so on. It is very important to begin right away.

If you notice you have difficulty reading your college texts, look ahead to Chapter 6 *now*. If taking notes is a problem for you, look ahead to Chapter 5 *now*.

Often students find themselves enrolled in a class that is too difficult, too easy, or not relevant to them or their program of study. If this happens to you, consult your advisor or counselor at once. If you wait even a couple of weeks, it will be too late to add a class in the place of one you want to drop.

Now that you have prepared yourself for the first week of college, you are probably still nervous. Don't worry about it. Everyone else is nervous, too. *The difference is you have a plan and some answers to help you get through it!* Your first week will probably be one of the most challenging, frustrating, confusing, hectic, tiring, exhilarating, and stimulating weeks of your life. Everyone's first week of college is (even ours was!). Hang in there. Your life will even out. Stick with this book. You'll learn a lot, and you'll have the tools you need to succeed. You are on your way!

2 ASSESSING YOUR LEARNING STYLE

Tips

1. Discover what your preferred learning style is and adapt what you are learning to that learning style.
2. Add to your learning repertoire by practicing other learning styles.
3. Choose the learning style best suited for each learning task.
4. Become a "superlearner" by discovering the most effective ways, times, and places for you to learn.

A Left-Brained Overview

I. Discovering Your Learning Patterns
  A. Formal assessments
    1. Myers-Briggs Type Inventory
    2. Kolb's Learning Style Inventory
    3. Learning and Study Strategies Inventory (LASSI)
  B. Informal assessments
    1. Informal speaking style assessment
    2. Formal speaking style assessment
    3. Listening style assessment
II. Personal Learning Style Summary

A Right-Brained Overview

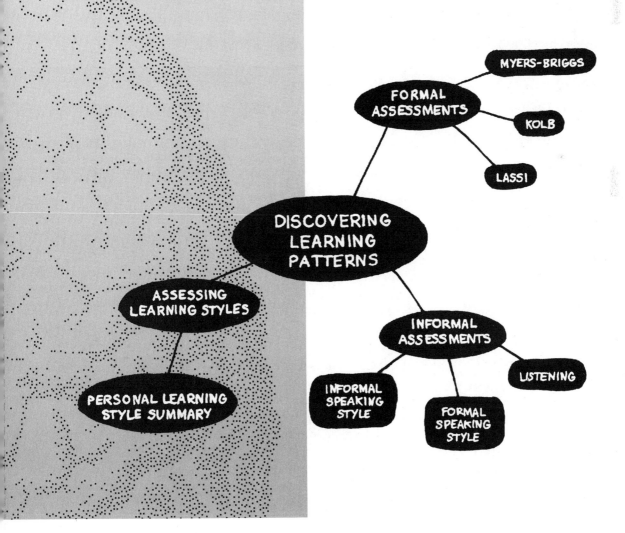

MYERS-BRIGGS

FORMAL ASSESSMENTS

KOLB

LASSI

DISCOVERING LEARNING PATTERNS

ASSESSING LEARNING STYLES

PERSONAL LEARNING STYLE SUMMARY

INFORMAL ASSESSMENTS

INFORMAL SPEAKING STYLE

FORMAL SPEAKING STYLE

LISTENING

You're a little nervous about your ability to handle college-level coursework. You're not sure what your preferred learning style is. In fact, you're not even sure what learning styles are. In this chapter we'll give you some tools to discover what your learning style is. Keep in mind, however, that there is no one best way to discover your preferred learning style. You can use the descriptions and definitions of the various patterns given in the Prologue and simply decide which one you use the most based on what you know about yourself and how you learn. You may choose to take a more formal, standardized inventory such as those listed below. Or, you can take the more informal assessments provided later in this chapter.

IS THIS YOU?

FORMAL LEARNING STYLE ASSESSMENTS

Several standardized inventories will provide you with information about how you process information and what learning environments you work best in. If you wish to explore this subject further, consider taking one of the following inventories. Note that these are not the only inventories that assess learning styles; check at your college's counseling, testing, or advising centers to see what's available.

The **Myers-Briggs Type Inventory** provides you with an eight-element personality type profile, rating you on four continuums. Two of these continuums provide information about preferred learning styles and work environments.

David Kolb's **Learning Style Inventory** categorizes you into one of four types: diverger, converger, assimilator, or accommodator. Kolb's initial groups tell you something about how

EXERCISE 2.1

TAKING A FORMAL ASSESSMENT

Take one or more standardized or more formal learning style assessments. What new insights did you get? Does the assessment evaluation surprise you? How can you use this information to make yourself a more successful student?

you like to learn, what form you prefer information in, and what type of study environment you prefer.

The **Learning and Study Strategies Inventory (LASSI)** measures your use of learning and study strategies in ten areas: attitude, motivation, time management, anxiety, concentration, information processing, selection of main ideas, study aids, self-testing, and test strategies. This inventory pinpoints areas in which you may need improvement and often suggests ways to begin improving.[1]

Produced by ACT, **ASSET placement tests** are used by a number of schools to assess student knowledge in English, reading, and math. A companion test is a study skills inventory that compares your learning and study strategies to those of groups of college students. This inventory focuses on your use and application of learning skills rather than your style, but it can give you insight into your patterns of academic learning.

INFORMAL LEARNING STYLE ASSESSMENTS

To get a sense of your preferred learning style, for each of the following statements, circle the letter corresponding to the response that describes you best. Scoring instructions are provided at the end of the exercise.

1. When trying to study, I'm often distracted:
   a. by what I see around me.
   b. by sounds.
   c. by how I feel physically.
2. When I begin to understand a difficult concept, I'm most likely to say:
   a. "It's clear to me now."
   b. "*That* rings a bell."
   c. "I've got a handle on it."
3. In school I learn best:
   a. from my textbooks.
   b. from class lectures.
   c. in laboratories, discussions, or activity classes.
4. If I need directions to find a particular place, I:
   a. want to be given instructions to read.
   b. want to be told how to get there.
   c. want to follow someone there the first time I go.
5. I remember the last party I went to best:
   a. by where the party was, what the room looked like, who was there, and what I was wearing.

    b. by whom I went with, what our conversation was about, what music was played, and what the occasion was (birthday, ball game party, and so on).

    c. by what I ate, drank, and did while I was there and by how I got there and how I got home.

6. I prefer to spend my weekends and free time:

    a. doing what I want to do whenever I want to do it.

    b. making a list of what I have to do and checking things off the list as I do them.

7. When an instructor gives out an assignment, I prefer:

    a. to know the exact requirements for completing the assignment—when it is due, how long it should be, how to format it, and so on.

    b. to have some freedom to set the standards, figure out different ways to do the assignment, and turn it in when I please.

8. When planning a party, I:

    a. make lists of whom I'll invite, what food and drink to serve, and what I need to do before the party.

    b. think about the type of party mood I want and then invite the right people to create it.

9. When I move into a new place, I:

    a. mentally see how the furniture can be arranged.

    b. draw out a floorplan before arranging the furniture.

10. When talking with a friend, I:

    a. understand what my friend is telling me mostly from the words spoken.

    b. get the message from my friend's facial expressions and gestures (that is, nonverbals) as well as his or her words.

11. In thinking about how I talk and write, the statement that describes me best is:

    a. I use very precise language to describe and explain what I am talking or writing about. I am very conscious of and careful with grammar and the meanings of words.

    b. When talking or writing, I use metaphors, similes, and lots of other figurative language. My communication style is descriptive, and maybe even poetic or emotional.

12. When solving a problem or learning a new concept or process, I:

    a. prefer to look at the parts and put things in step-by-step order.

    b. prefer to get a sense of the whole problem or concept first.

13. When I make up my mind about how I feel about an issue, I:

a. look at the facts, think about the issue logically and rationally, and then come to my conclusion.

b. often make up my mind based on emotion or intuition.

14. It is easy for me to see how things fit together in a pattern or relationship.

a. Yes.

b. No.

15. Generally I know what time it is.

a. Yes.

b. No.

Learning styles scoring and evaluation *Note:* This assessment is scored in two parts.

Part I: For items 1–5 total up the number of *a*, *b*, and *c* responses. A score with more *a* responses suggests that you process information visually. A score with more *b* responses suggests that you do more auditory processing. A score with more *c* responses suggests that you are a kinesthetic learner. If your final score falls between two indicators, say *a* and *c*, you are probably using two styles, visual and auditory, about equally.

Remember, no one processing style is better than another. It's just your habitual way of taking in and making sense of information. Also remember, however, that learning is easier and faster if you can process information in more than one style.

Part II: Based on the following number values for each of the responses for items 6–15, total up your score and divide by 10.

6.	a = 7	b = 1	11.	a = 1	b = 7
7.	a = 1	b = 5	12.	a = 3	b = 5
8.	a = 1	b = 5	13.	a = 1	b = 7
9.	a = 5	b = 3	14.	a = 7	b = 1
10.	a = 3	b = 5	15.	a = 3	b = 5

A score between 1 and 3.4 indicates that you function primarily in a left-brained mode while a score between 3.5 and 4.9 suggests that you use a combination of left- and right-brain functions. A score between 5 and 7 indicates that you are more of a right-brained processor.

Again, you may find it informative to review your responses. By doing so you can gain a better idea of typical left- and right-brain behaviors (the lower the number—generally 1 and 3—assigned the response, the more left-brained it is; the higher the number—generally 5 and 7—the more right-brained it is). You may discover that in a certain situation or environment

EXPERIMENTING WITH NEW LEARNING STYLES

Practice doing something differently than you ordinarily would in order to develop your skill in a nonhabitual learning pattern. For example, if you are a visual processor, try memorizing a list of terms by reciting them aloud. If you are an auditory processor, try creating a diagram or spidergram of a chapter's main and supporting points while you recite the points. If you tend to function more right-brained, then list the steps in a sequence, take detailed notes during a lecture, or analyze something by breaking it down into smaller components. If you usually process left-brained, then work at comprehending a concept by looking first at the big picture. Doing this little by little will result in your having more options for completing academic assignments.

you tend to function in your left brain while a different situation or place causes you to switch to your right brain. Remember, neither mode is preferable. Rather, what's important is that you match each hemisphere to the demands of the job. For example, since lecture note-taking is a left-brained task, it works best if you are in your "left-brain mode" when doing it.

LEFT- AND RIGHT-BRAINED COMMUNICATION ASSESSMENTS

Use the following assessments to discover more about how you function when you communicate. You can also use these as guides for assessing your instructors in order to see how your two styles fit. If you find yourself in a class with an instructor whose style clashes with your own, this will give you some specifics to consider when trying to understand and communicate with that individual.[2]

Informal Speaking Style Assessment

Complete the following to determine how you talk with and interact with friends, family, or acquaintances.

When talking with someone, I: (*Check all items that apply.*)
_____ 1. dislike being interrupted.
_____ 2. sometimes leave out details in order to get to the final point.
_____ 3. prefer to do so over the phone.
_____ 4. prefer to do so face-to-face.
_____ 5. plan what I'm going to say with a purpose or an objective in mind.
_____ 6. sometimes leave sentences unfinished.

_____ 7. start over if distracted or interrupted.

_____ 8. sometimes find myself stuttering or using imprecise vocabulary.

_____ 9. plan what I'm going to say with a practical application in mind.

_____ 10. consider a number of different elements.

Informal speaking style scoring and evaluation Score 1 point for each odd-numbered item you checked and 2 points for each even-numbered item you checked. Total up your score. The lower the score, the more of a left-brained talker you are; the higher the score, the more of a right-brained talker you are.

Formal Speaking Style Assessment

Complete the following to determine how you communicate when giving a speech, making a formal presentation, or simply talking in class. *Note:* You can use this assessment to evaluate your instructors' styles as well.

When communicating formally, I: (*Check all items that apply.*)

_____ 1. am articulate and formal. (1)

_____ 2. use metaphors and other figurative language. (9)

_____ 3. reword points. (5)

_____ 4. use emotional language. (7)

_____ 5. deal in facts and figures. (1)

_____ 6. include personal examples. (9)

_____ 7. sometimes stutter or lose my train of thought. (5)

_____ 8. use few nonverbal gestures. (1)

_____ 9. relate the topic to my listeners' interests. (3)

_____ 10. am disorganized. (9)

Formal speaking style scoring and evaluation First, count the number of items you checked. Then add up the numbers given in parentheses after each of the items you checked. Now divide the point total by the number of items you checked. A low score indicates left-brained speaking characteristics while a higher one indicates right-brained speaking characteristics. A score in the mid-range suggests that you are using both left- and right-brained characteristics. If you evaluate your instructors, you can use this information to better understand how the class is being structured and organized. If you discover that you are very different from one of your instructors, this can suggest ways to adapt.

Listening Style Assessment

Complete the following to determine how you listen to others talking, whether it be in a social situation, with friends or family, or in a formal environment such as a lecture.

When listening to a speaker, I: (*Check all items that apply.*)

_____ 1. find technical data boring. (8)

_____ 2. analyze both verbal and nonverbal messages. (3)

_____ 3. need to understand all the details to make sure I've got it right. (5)

_____ 4. ask questions. (2)

_____ 5. don't like ambiguous or emotional language. (1)

_____ 6. think about how to apply or use the speaker's ideas. (4)

_____ 7. am concerned about how the audience is receiving the speaker. (6)

_____ 8. have difficulty comprehending technical information. (7)

_____ 9. often am suspicious of the speaker. (9)

Listening style scoring and evaluation First, count the number of items you checked. Then add up the numbers given in parentheses after each of the items you checked. Now divide the point total by the number of items you checked. A low score suggests left-brained listening characteristics while a higher number indicates right-brained listening characteristics. A score in the mid-range suggests that you are using both left- and right-brained listening traits. You may also find it helpful to look at the numbers in parentheses of the individual items you checked. The higher-numbered items are right-brained characteristics while lower-numbered items are more left-brained.

EXERCISE 2.3

EVALUATING COMMUNICATION STYLES

Evaluate the communication style of one of your instructors. Does this match your communication style? If not, what are some specific ways you can adapt your listening style to better understand your instructor? For example, does your instructor use facts and figures to communicate or does he or she use figurative language? Does this instructor repeat points to emphasize them or use certain nonverbal gestures for emphasis?

Supplemental exercise: Evaluate the communication style of a public speaker, a politician, or a preacher. What are specific characteristics of this individual's style? Is he or she effective? Why or why not?

PERSONAL LEARNING STYLE SUMMARY

Take some of the assessments on learning styles discussed in the Prologue and in this chapter. Record the results here and use it to help identify the most effective study place, time, and environment for yourself. Note that as you learn more approaches to studying, your habits and preferences may change. Thus you may find it interesting to answer these questions again at the end of the quarter, semester, or year.

1. I am a(n) _____ visual _____ auditory _____ kinesthetic processor.

2. My score on items 1–5 of the informal learning style assessment was _____ .

3. I tend to be a _____ left-brained _____ combination _____ right-brained person.

4. My score on items 6–15 of the informal learning style assessment was _____ .

5. My score on the informal speaking style assessment was _____ , making me _____ .

6. My score on the formal speaking style assessment was _____ , making me _____ .

7. My score on the listening style assessment was _____ , making me _____ .

8. My scores on any other learning style assessments I've taken:
   a. MBTI _____
   b. Kolb _____
   c. LASSI _____
   d. Other _____

9. I am most intellectually alert in the (*circle one*) (a) early morning, (b) mid-morning, (c) early afternoon, (d) late afternoon, (e) early evening, (f) late evening, (g) midnight-to-dawn hours. This is your Prime Internal Time. (*Tip:* Schedule some of your intellectually challenging reading or study during a portion of your Prime Internal Time.)

10. I am least intellectually alert in the (*circle one*) (a) early morning, (b) mid-morning, (c) early afternoon, (d) late afternoon, (e) early evening, (f) late evening, (g) midnight-to-dawn hours. This is your Prime External Time. (*Tip:* Schedule some routine or non-intellectually demanding academic work during a portion of your Prime External Time.)

11. The best place for me to study at home is _____ _____ .

12. The best place for me to study on campus is _____ _____ .

FINDING YOUR OPTIMAL STUDY ENVIRONMENT

Locate two or three good places for you to study on your campus. Pay attention to how much studying you get done there compared with when you study in a less positive environment. Do the same thing for where you live.

Next, figure out the best times of day and days of the week for you to study. You may discover that *when* as well as *what* you are studying makes a difference.

Finally, develop a clear idea of your most effective study environment—at a desk, in a comfortable chair, inside, outside, with other people, alone, silent as a tomb, and so on.

13. The worst place for me to study at home is _____
    _____ .

14. The worst place for me to study on campus is _____
    _____ .

15. The best day of the week for me to study is _____
    _____ .

16. The worst day of the week for me to study is _____
    _____ .

17. I study best when there is (a) dead quiet, (b) quiet, instrumental music playing in the background, (c) rock music blaring away, or (d) _____ .

18. I study best when I am (a) alone, (b) with one or two friends, (c) with a group, or (d) _____ .

19. I remember best what I study when I (a) can see it in picture or diagram form, (b) can recite the information aloud or to myself, or (c) use it or do it physically.

20. When learning new information, ideas, or concepts, I remember best when I (a) understand the parts or pieces and can put stuff into a logical order, or (b) begin with the big picture and then study and understand the various pieces.

Notes

[1]Claire E. Weinstein, David R. Palmer, and Ann C. Schulte, *Learning and Study Strategies Inventory* (Clearwater, FL: H & H, 1987).

[2]Left- and right-brained communications assessment developed using information from Chapter 10 of Jacquelyn Wonder and Priscilla Donovan's *Whole Brain Thinking* (New York: Ballantine Books, 1984).

3

MANAGING YOUR TIME

Tips

1. Use the 168 hours in a week wisely.
2. Match your brain dominance pattern to your time management plan.
3. Set goals, make plans, and then act.
4. Use a calender <u>always!</u>
5. Make and follow a master schedule.
6. Use a daily planner or "to do" list.
7. Apply accepted time management principles.
8. Deal with procrastination.

A Left-Brained Overview

I. Time and College
   A. Time equalizes people—168 hours in a week
   B. Time needs of types of students
   C. Goal is balance
   D. Brain dominance and time
      1. Left like structure, routine, deadlines
      2. Right like variety, innovation, flexibility
II. Evaluating Your Present Use of Time
III. Applying Time Management Principles
   A. Calenders
   B. Master schedules
   C. Daily planners and "to-do" lists
   D. Weekly schedules
   E. Project organizers
   F. Foundations of time management principles
   G. Seven principles of time and learning
   H. Single-session study planners
   I. Effective ways of reviewing
IV. Procrastination
   A. Why people procrastinate
   B. How to deal with procrastination

A Right-Brained Overview

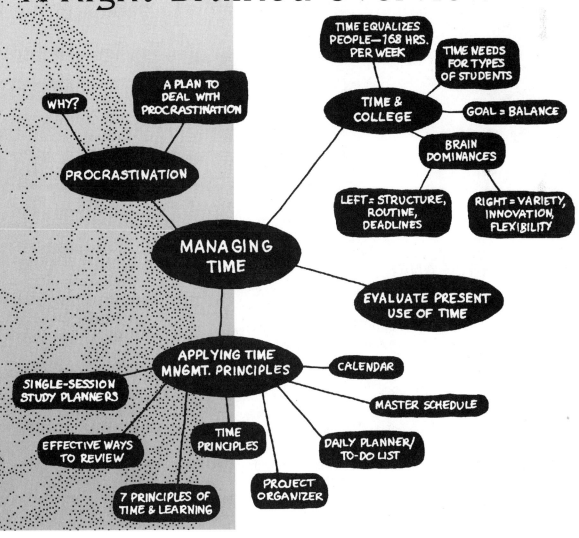

TIME EQUALIZES PEOPLE—168 HRS. PER WEEK

TIME NEEDS FOR TYPES OF STUDENTS

TIME & COLLEGE

GOAL = BALANCE

BRAIN DOMINANCES

LEFT = STRUCTURE, ROUTINE, DEADLINES

RIGHT = VARIETY, INNOVATION, FLEXIBILITY

WHY?

A PLAN TO DEAL WITH PROCRASTINATION

PROCRASTINATION

MANAGING TIME

EVALUATE PRESENT USE OF TIME

APPLYING TIME MNGMT. PRINCIPLES

CALENDAR

MASTER SCHEDULE

DAILY PLANNER/ TO-DO LIST

PROJECT ORGANIZER

TIME PRINCIPLES

SINGLE-SESSION STUDY PLANNERS

EFFECTIVE WAYS TO REVIEW

7 PRINCIPLES OF TIME & LEARNING

You think college life is great. You love all the things there are to do—go to the gym, hang out in the student union, join clubs, go to parties. And you love it that no one tells you when to get up in the morning or forces you to go to class or nags you to do your home-work. But you're starting to wonder how you'll ever find the time to do everything you want to do, inside and outside the classroom. Indeed, time management is crucial to college success. In this chapter we'll show you how to manage your time so as to get the most out of your college experience.

IS THIS YOU?

ACHIEVING BALANCE

Time is one of the great equalizers for people. Each of us has exactly 168 hours per week to "spend." And no matter how rich or poor, able or disabled, gifted or average, or whatever, we all have to decide how to use those hours.

The phrase *time management* is actually somewhat mislead-ing. The real issue is *self-management* in relation to time issues. At no time in your life is managing self and managing time more important than during college. For many traditional-age college students, the newfound freedom of being on campus can be overwhelming. After years of being told what to do and when to do it by parents, teachers, and principals, many new college students enjoy the new freedoms of college to excess. For re-entry or adult college students, the demands of an al-ready full life are significantly increased by the pursuit of higher education. In addition to home, work, and family responsibilities, these students must deal with the rigors of college coursework. And even though they may be more academically advanced than beginning students, these students face the added pressure of familiarizing themselves with a new environment. Athletes face the pressures of heavy practice, competition, and travel schedules in addition to studying and maintaining grades for eligibility. Students on scholarship also must maintain a certain grade point average to keep their funding for school. Disabled students also have additional time pressures. For instance, blind and visually impaired students often need to have books, assignments, and readings taped for and/or read to them. Some hearing-impaired and deaf students require the services of an interpreter, or need to arrange for amplification devices or note-taking assistance, which is time-consuming. Some orthopedically impaired students need to allot extra time for transportation and for writing and other academic tasks. Many learning disabled students take longer to master school material and often work with tutors. Married students have family responsibilities, as do students who live at home with their parents. Students who live on their own have home management duties to juggle. In short, all groups of students have some special needs or concerns regarding time and college success.

College and college campuses provide a wealth of opportunities for stimulating activities and company outside of the classroom. The student union, recreation center, student center, and mall often prove much more appealing than the classroom or library. To be sure, college is not just academic work; without some time spent on social and extracurricular activities, the college experience will be greatly diminished and compromised. But the student who spends too much time on such activities risks waking up one day as an *ex*-student.

The goal is to achieve *balance*: to have time for fun, for study, for physical, emotional, spiritual, and intellectual growth and change. It is possible to have time for all of these—but not every day. The key is to have a balanced life.

BRAIN DOMINANCE AND TIME MANAGEMENT

There is no one right way to manage time, to make out a schedule, or to use a calendar. Most time management texts use a left-brained approach to managing time. Given that left-brained people tend to be better oriented to clock and calendar time, most time management techniques seem more aligned to the left side of the brain. However, using the right, creative side of the brain can give you the balance needed to effectively manage time. Left-brain-dominant students will enjoy and excel at the aspects of time management that involve structure, routine, and deadlines. Right-brain-dominant students will enjoy and excel at the aspects of time management that involve variety, innovation, flexibility, and creativity. The techniques in this chapter are presented from both the left and right perspectives. Try both techniques for a while and see how you can fit them together to a balanced, whole-brained time management system.

EVALUATING YOUR PRESENT USE OF TIME

Our first task is to assess how you presently use time. Once you know where the time is currently going, you can make decisions on how to spend your time in the future.

Goals, Plans, and Action

You need to assess how you currently use your time for many reasons. In order to manage time successfully, you need to *want* to succeed in managing time. In addition to learning and growing, most college students endeavor to earn a high grade point average, or GPA. But these three letters also stand for the three key ingredients in time management:

> **G**oal
> **P**lan
> **A**ction + Attitude

Once you have established a *goal*, you need a *plan* to reach this goal, but to do this you need some information. The information acquired by keeping a time log or time wheel of your days and hours will help you make out your time plan. Once you have a plan that will work for you, you can put this plan into *action* by having a positive *attitude*. Together, the goals, the plans, and the actions and attitudes—the GPA of time management—lead to success!

Imagine planning your ideal school day. You will have time to get everywhere you need to be and time to accomplish all the necessary tasks. You will have the right amount of stimulation, and your day will progress at a comfortable pace for you. These elements comprise your time management goals.

Time Circles and Time Logs

Your goals regarding time can be realized if you evaluate your present use of time as part of the time management process. Although there are a number of ways to do this, we will focus on two: (1) the time circle, a right-brained approach to time use evaluation, and (2) the time log, a left-brained approach to time use evaluation.

Time circles Using the time circle shown in Figure 3.1, keep track of how you spend your time each day for four days. Stop once in the morning, once in the afternoon, and once before bed, and color in the appropriate circle hours for each activity. This time circle is much more effective when you use different colors to show various activities. Do *not* fill this chart out in advance. Note, too, that this will not yield a schedule to follow; rather, it will simply give you a realistic picture of where your time is currently going.

At the end of each day, evaluate your use of time. Add up the hours spent on each activity. Make notes or code specific sections to indicate areas where you think you are spending too little time, too much time, and about the right amount of time. When, where, and how did you waste time this day? How do you want tomorrow to differ?

Time logs Using the time log shown in Figure 3.2, keep track of how you spend your time each day for four days. Stop at each mealtime and before bed, and fill out the chart. This time log will help you see where the time has been spent. Do *not* fill this out in advance. Again, this will not result in a schedule to follow, but rather give you a realistic picture of

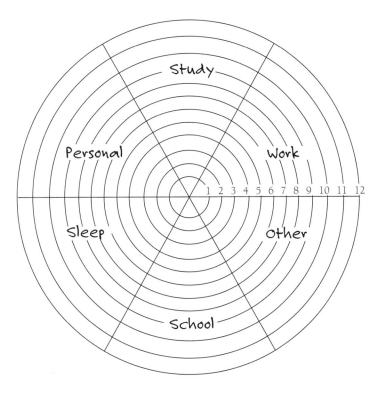

Figure 3.1
Time Circle

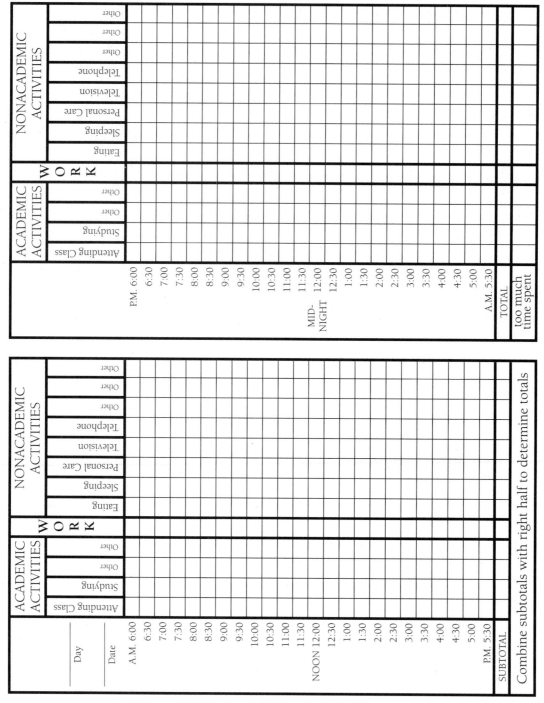

Figure 3.2
Time Log

where your time is currently going. At the end of each day, evaluate your use of time. Add up the hours spent in each category. Make notes or code specific time blocks to indicate areas where you think you are spending too little time, too much time, and about the right amount of time. When, where, and

EVALUATING YOUR TIME LOGS AND CIRCLES

Now that you have gathered your "raw data," you need to evaluate it. In your journal, on a piece of paper, or on 3 × 5 cards, complete the following statements.

In looking back over the past four days:

1. I wish I had spent more time _____
   _____ .

2. I wish I had spent less time _____
   _____ .

3. I avoided studying when I was supposed to be studying by _____
   _____ .

4. I had no idea I spend so little time _____
   _____ .

5. I had no idea I spend so much time _____
   _____ .

6. If I could change one thing about how I use my time, it would be
   _____ .

7. One thing I would not change is _____
   _____ .

8. I hope tomorrow will be different from today in terms of _____
   _____ .

9. I hope tomorrow will be the same as today in terms of _____
   _____ .

10. The most interesting thing I learned about myself in terms of time
    management is _____
    _____ .

Group activity: Discuss the responses to the items in a small group. How do their responses differ? What can you learn from how they spend their time?

how did you waste time this day? How do you want tomorrow to differ?

The whole-brained approach Once again, every day for four days keep track of how you spend your time. This time, however, for two days, one of which should be a weekend day, fill out the time log. For two other days, one of which should be a weekend day, color in the time circle. At the end of the four days, ask yourself which approach you liked better. Which felt more comfortable? Which was easier to complete? Did you learn something from one that you did not from the other? The answers to these questions may help you evaluate your brain dominance as it relates to time management.

Task (e.g., reading, writing, solving problems)	Study Date and Class	Time Begun and Finished (A.M./P.M.)	Total Time Used (in minutes)	Total No. of Pages Completed	Concentration Span (in minutes)	Study Place	Evaluation of Study Session

Figure 3.3
Rate of Study

CHAPTER 3   MANAGING YOUR TIME

Your Rate of Study

The detective work is not over. Through your time logs and circles you should now have a sense of where your time is going each day. Now we need to zero in on your schoolwork and determine how much studying you can do during a given period of time. It is vital to be realistic about how much time you need to allot for daily and weekly study, and conversely how much time you will have for nonacademic activities.

To begin, identify how much you accomplish during your current study sessions by filling in the chart in Figure 3.3. Be honest with yourself. No one is going to evaluate this section except you.

Now that you have determined your rate of study, you need to figure out how much time you need to spend studying for each class. An old myth states that a student should study 2 hours outside of class for every hour spent in class. Most students, however, have found that this rule of thumb doesn't work very well—some classes require much more while others seem to require less. For example, engineering and English are both 3-credit-hour classes. The standard rule of thumb says you would need to study 6 hours a week for both these classes (3 × 2 = 6), but most of our students have found that they need to devote more study hours for each class. On the other hand, 6 hours was about right for a sociology class, while a biology class required 10 or more hours.

Therefore you need a better way to determine how much time you will need to devote to study each week. Complete the chart in Figure 3.4 to estimate the number of weekly study hours you will need.

APPLYING TIME MANAGEMENT PRINCIPLES

The first part of your time-sleuthing process is now finished. You have determined how you currently spend your time, how long it takes you to study for each of your classes, and how much time you will need to study each week. Now you can begin to use specific time management tools: (1) calendars, (2) weekly and master schedules, (3) daily planners or to-do lists, and (4) project organizers. In addition, you can apply principles of time management to single-session studying and to reviewing.

Calendars

A calendar is a vital tool for college and lifelong success. Calendars come in all sorts of styles and price ranges, but any good calendar will contain the following:

- Enough space to write at least six to eight lines in for every day

(1) Classes (list in priority order)	(2) Grade Desired	(3) Type of Assignment Normally Given[a]	(4) Rate of Work per Hour[b]	(5) Average Amount of Weekly Assignments	(6) Minimum No. of First-Exposure Hrs. Needed Weekly[c]	(7) Estimated Weekly Review Time[d]	(8) Weekly Total Study Hours Needed (add 6 and 7)

[a]For example, reading, problem-solving, essay writing.
[b]For example, 20 pages per hour or 5 problems per hour.
[c]In other words, the number of hours needed to read the material or complete the problems.
[d]For example, to review the main ideas in the reading and make spidergrams, or review the formulas for the problems and the concepts behind them.

TOTAL →

Figure 3.4
Estimation of Weekly Study Hours

- A place to record names, addresses, and phone numbers
- A place to write in (or staple in) a class schedule

In addition, the calendar will be small enough that you can carry it with you at all times. Remember, the amount of *money* you spend on the calendar doesn't matter at all, but the amount

KEEPING A CALENDAR

Purchase and fill out a calendar listing all important dates for the semester—both academic and extracurricular—as well as your instructors' names, phone numbers, and office hours and locations, and classmates' names and phone numbers. Try color-coding your entries.

of *time* you spend using your calendar and referring to it can be the key to successful time management.

The first item you are creating in this calendar is a *semester overview* or *plan*. Here you will record important dates—tests, papers, and so on—for all your classes. This semester overview can help you both achieve success and prevent unpleasant surprises such as discovering you have a term paper due in two days. The semester overview enables you to look ahead and see what you have due the entire semester. Depending on your preferred learning style and brain dominance, you might also want to list these major dates on a wall calendar, on a separate sheet of paper, or inside your notebooks, so you can look ahead and see what is due and add to them easily. Some students like to fill out a month-at-a-glance type of calendar in addition to the listed due dates on individual pages.

You may think that your coloring days ended in kindergarten—or at least with your time circle—but coloring in a calendar or time planner can be very helpful. A good way to begin to sort your many tasks is to take your syllabi from all your classes and choose a color to represent each class. Then go through your calendar, marking down (using the chosen colors for each class) all major due dates, test dates, assignment dates, and so forth for each class for the entire semester. Use your favorite color to record dates for social events, parties, games, trips, and the like.

Next, in the address portion of the calendar, copy the names, phone numbers, and office hours and office locations of each instructor, and the name and phone number of at least one other student in each of your classes. Carry your calendars with you everywhere you go during the day. Every time an assignment is given or an appointment is made, it should be listed in the calendar. The key to successful time management is regularly referring to, checking, and listing items in your calendar. No commitments or appointments should be made without first referring to the calendar. You need to get in the habit of looking ahead to see what is coming up.

Master Schedules

Many new students face the daily challenge of waking up and trying to figure out where they're supposed to be that day. Since many class schedules are staggered—that is, classes meet on Mondays, Wednesdays, and Fridays, or on Tuesdays and Thursdays—it can be a struggle to establish some sense of rhythm to your days. When should you study or go to the gym or eat meals? Students with children need to balance classes and study time with child care and parenting duties.

The key to getting control of your days is creating and using a master schedule. A master schedule is like a time management road map that shows you exactly where you need to go and how to get there.

In creating a master schedule, it's helpful to think in terms of a layer cake. The first layer is made up of your regular weekly commitments: classes, meetings, jobs, family obligations, and so on. The second layer contains the things that need to be done daily or weekly but whose time frames are flexible. For example, studying, sleeping, eating, and exercising all must be done daily, but you may have some control over when each can be accomplished. The frosting, the sweetest part of the cake, represents your free or discretionary time. This includes time for recreation, family and social activities, and plain old relaxation. It's important that you plan for these activities, and not simply include them only if you have time or have to spend less time on other activities.

Like a great cake, a good master schedule has just the right blend of ingredients; too much of one or too little of another and your schedule—and your life—will suffer. Building a good master schedule ensures that you will have time for the "frosting" or the free time to spend performing discretionary activities. Most students have a great deal of flexibility in choosing what activities will take place where and when on their master schedules. You can enjoy your discretionary time to the fullest if you know that the essential tasks of the day have been accomplished or that the time is slated for them to be accomplished.

It is important to note that you have some freedom to tailor your master schedule to your own needs and preferences; no two will be alike. Left-brain-dominant students will tend to prefer a master schedule that is highly structured, orderly, and predictable, one that stays the same from day to day as much as possible. Right-brain-dominants prefer a more flexible master schedule, one that allows variety, change, and movement from task to task. Both approaches are fine; you need to find out what works best for you.

But how do you go about creating a workable master schedule? Figures 3.5 and 3.6 show two sample master schedules. To start filling out your schedule, refer back to your time wheel or time log to see where you were spending your time. From this:

1. Fill in classes, work, and any other commitments for which you have no control over the time they occur.
2. Fill in sleep, meals, exercise, personal care, and all those items that must be done daily but for which you have control over the time.

A.M.	Sunday	Monday	Tuesday	Wednesday	Thursday	Friday	Saturday
6-7			D r e s s B r e a k f a s t				
7-8		Dress Breakfast	Psychology	BIO Lecture	Psychology	Dress Breakfast	
8-9		STUDY	↓ Prep Math	↓	↓ Prep Math	STUDY	Extra Study
9-10		STUDY	Math		Math	STUDY	Time, if Needed
10-11		English	↓	English	↓	English	
11-12		Freshman Seminar		Freshman Seminar		Freshman Seminar	
P.M. 12-1	←		L	U	N	C	H	→
1-2		Review today's notes (30 min)	Prep for BIO lab	Review class Notes	Prep for BIO lab	Review class Notes	
2-3	Extra Study	STUDY	BIO	STUDY	BIO	STUDY	
3-4	Time, if Needed	STUDY	LAB	STUDY	LAB	STUDY	
4-5			Review class Notes		Review class Notes		
5-6	Plan for Next Week	←	E X E R C I S E			→	
6-7		←	D I N N E R			→	
7-8		← S t u d y M a t h →				G o	
8-9		Extra Study Time ← →				I	
9-10						N G	
10-11						O U	
11-12	←	S L E E P			→	T	
A.M. 12-1							
1-2							

Figure 3.5
Sample Master Schedule

3. Refer to your estimation of weekly study hours and fill in study time for each class. You may choose simply to block out general study time or you may prefer to designate specific times to study for each of your classes.

A.M.	Sunday	Monday	Tuesday	Wednesday	Thursday	Friday	Saturday
6-7		← J O G G I N G →					
7-8		← Get ready for class, eat, walk to class →					
8-9		English	Prep for Fr. Engineer	English	Prep for Fr. Engineer	English	Green-Peace Volunteer
9-10		Environ. Science	Freshman Engineering	Environ. Science	Freshman Engineering	Environ. Science	
10-11		Rev Leacture Notes Break	↓	Note Review Break	↓	Note Review Break	
11-12 P.M.		Freshman Seminar	LUNCH	Freshman Seminar	LUNCH	Freshman Seminar	
12-1		LUNCH	Math	LUNCH	Math	LUNCH	
1-2		Env. Sci Lab	↓	Fr. Engineer LAB Prep	↓	Review all Lecture notes for week Prepare for next week	
2-3		↓	Note Review Break	Fr. Engineer LAB	Note Review Break		
3-4		Break	S T U D Y		S T U D Y		
4-5		S T U D Y		↓			
5-6							
6-7		← D I N N E R →					
7-8		S T U D Y	S T U D Y	S T U D Y		S	S
8-9						O	O
9-10		Watch Northern Exposure			Watch LA Law	C	C
10-11		← B e d t i m e →				I	I
11-12 A.M.						A	A
12-1						L	L
1-2							

Figure 3.6
Sample Master Schedule

Note that it is best to place short study sessions *before* lecture-type classes whenever possible and to have review times after all classes if possible to review your notes and create study questions for the class material. Once review times are scheduled, place longer study sessions throughout the week. Count the study hours to ensure that you have listed as

CREATING YOUR MASTER SCHEDULE

Using the samples in Figures 3.5 and 3.6 as models, create your own master schedule. Refer to your time log and wheel as needed.

many study hours for each class as you indicated you needed on your estimation of weekly study hours in Figure 3.4.

Once these essential events are listed on your master schedule, color in your free times. You may need to redo this schedule a number of times to ensure that your free time is placed where you ideally want it.

Many students find it helpful to use several different colors on their master schedule. Even left-brained students, for whom color is less of a cue for learning, can benefit from using color. One option is to distinguish activities by color, such as all work items in yellow, all school items in green, and so on. Another option is to use one color for each of your classes. For example, if you chose red for biology, biology class times, biology laboratory times, biology study times, biology study group times, and biology tutorial sessions all would be recorded in red.

Once you have completed your master schedule, copy it into your calendar or staple it to the front cover of your calendar. Pay attention for the next few weeks to see how it works. Jot down in your calendar the days that went well and the days that didn't. After about four weeks, revise this master schedule based on what you learned during your four-week trial period.

Daily Planner and To-Do Lists

You now have established your goals and gathered information to make out a plan (your master schedule). However, the hardest part of time management is also the most essential—the *action/attitude* step. The way to make the action step reality is by using a daily planner.

To make out a daily planner, you must combine your calendar and your master schedule on a daily basis. Some students do this before going to bed each night. Right-brain-oriented students especially, who like to see the "big picture," find creating a daily planner the night before to be very helpful. Some left-brained students, by contrast, prefer to make out their list each morning. It does not matter when you make out your daily plan, but it is vital that you do it on a regular basis and that you refer to it and follow it.

A variation is to make out seven to-do lists, one for each day of the coming week, on Sundays, and then fill in the details each morning. This combines a daily planner with a weekly overview.

Weekly Schedules and Project Organizers

All students have killer weeks. For example, you may discover you have four exams in one week or two term papers due the same day; perhaps your daughter's dance recital is the same day as your major presentation in communication; or you may have to be out of town the weekend before you have to turn in a project worth 50 percent of your grade. Unfortunately most students don't become aware of such killer weeks until the week arrives, and then *it is too late*. If you can discover your killer weeks in advance, you are already in a position of power. Armed with foreknowledge of these tough, "time crunch" weeks, you can plan how to cope using two time management techniques: the weekly schedule and the project organizers.

The weekly schedule is a compilation of seven daily planners. It gives you the chance to look at the week as a whole and determine what slots of discretionary time should be allotted to various school and life demands. The homework-oriented weekly planner shown in Figure 3.7 is an especially effective type of weekly planner.

Big assignments such as term papers or major presentations can seem insurmountable. However, by breaking the giant, seemingly undoable task into several smaller ones, it can be accomplished. The phrase *term paper* implies that the paper should take a "term" or semester to complete, just as the phrase *midterm exam* means that the exam will cover all the material presented in the course thus far. Most instructors assume that more dedicated students will actually spend time all semester working on a term paper. Students who try to complete a term paper in a couple of days often experience failure (that is why the paper is called a "term-paper" not a "two-nighter paper"). The process of completing a term project or paper can be made less daunting by following these steps:

1. Break down the project into smaller, time-specific parts.
2. Estimate how long each part will take.
3. Set a starting date for each part.
4. Monitor your progress regularly and often.
5. Complete each part and move on the next.
6. Reward yourself when you are done.

EXERCISE 3.4

USING A PROJECT ORGANIZER

Complete the blank project organizer form shown in Figure 3.9 for a term project due this semester. Your instructor may provide you with additional copies of this form.

Group activity: Explain your filled-out project organizer to a group of students. Listen as they explain theirs to you. Discuss what ideas you have in common, what ideas you can learn from your group mates, and how you can improve your project organizers.

CLASSES	MONDAY	TUESDAY	WEDNESDAY	THURSDAY	FRIDAY	SATURDAY	SUNDAY
OTHER ACADEMIC ACTIVITIES							
NONACADEMIC ACTIVITIES							

Figure 3.7
Homework Weekly Planner

MY GOALS FOR THIS WEEK: _____

Project Organizer

Course: **Literature**   Project: **Literature Critique**
                                                     5 pages
Due Date: **March 21**   Reward: **Go Ballooning**

Steps to Complete Major Project	Estimated Amount of Time Needed for This Step	Date to Begin This Step	Notes (about progress, needed info or things to do, problems, adjustments to be made)	Target Deadline for This Step	Reward
Read <u>Canticle for Leibowitz</u>	10-12 hours	2/12	Read 1 hr. at a time with a goal of 30 pages each time- TAKE NOTES	3/1	Dinner with friends & Movie
Brainstorm ideas for critique	1 hour	3/6	Use spidergram to begin to organize ideas	3/6	Pat on back
Organize Outline	30-60 minutes	3/7	Check for any needed information	3/8	Go out with friends
Collect any needed additional information	1-3 hours	3/10	Skip if not necessary	3/13	Movie
Write rough draft	3-5 hours	3/12	Do in sections i.e. so much at a time or 1 part of the outline	3/14	Buy new CD
Revise rough draft	1-3 hours	3/15	Again, do in small amounts of time or so many pages	3/17	Another pat on back
Print final copy	10 minutes	3/18	Word processors are wonderful!	3/18	
✸ Give self ✸ Reward ✸	48 hours	3/24	Yes!!!	3/25	Go away for weekend to go ballooning

Figure 3.8
Sample Filled-out Project Organizer

Figure 3.8 shows a sample project organizer for a term paper.

Time Management Principles

Once you have mastered general time management principles, you still need to manage your own study sessions. A sound approach is the *single-session study planner*, or "lesson plan" for study time. These help you plan what and when to

Course: _____ Project: _____

Due date: _____ Reward: _____

Steps to Complete Project	Estimated Amount of Time Needed for This Step	Date to Begin This Step	Notes (about progress, needed info or things to do, problems, adjustments to be made)	Target Deadline for This Step	Reward

Figure 3.9
Sample Blank Project Organizer

study. Because you study for only a few hours at a time, you will be more successful learning how to tailor time management principles to your personal style.

The time management principles for study make sense when applied to the single-session study planners. These principles include the five W's of time management:

- **Who**—Study only with those who support you and your goals. Study dates may be fun, but if you have to come home and study after them, perhaps you need to study alone or with individuals who share your academic goals and attitudes.

- **What**—Study your hardest, least-liked subjects first. Your attitude will improve, because you will get it over with and be able to have a more enjoyable session. Also, by studying your toughest subjects when you are freshest and most alert, you should retain more information and learn with greater ease. Finally, after you've studied for some time, you won't be faced with your worst subject, and thus you'll be less likely to procrastinate.

- **When**—Study during your peak functioning times. Each person has what is called an "internal body clock" or a *circadian rhythm*. This body clock allows us to have peak functioning times during the day called **prime internal time (PIT)** when intellectual abilities are high and **prime external time (PET)**[1] when our bodies and minds rebuild. It is vital to determine when your PITs and PETs occur and to schedule study times accordingly. The best way to do this is to spend a few days keeping track of when you feel most intellectually alert and when you feel intellectually least alert and unable to concentrate. Some people are night owls who enjoy working and are most creative into the night; others are morning people who rise early ready to function but who lose peak abilities later in the day. The key is not to waste your PIT folding laundry, watching TV, or doing errands—these can be effectively accomplished during your PET. Save your PIT for study.

- **Where**—Study in the best possible environment. This is as important as studying during your optimal times. The main issue in choosing a place to study is to find one place and study there regularly, whether it be your room, the library, the student union, or wherever. We are all creatures of habit. If you get in the habit of having effective study sessions at a particular place, just being there can help improve concentration and reduce study procrastination. The ideal study environment is maintained by regular practice. Develop a study preparation ritual whereby you sit in the same place, prepare your favorite beverage, wear a comfortable sweater, and so on. This practice will program your body to have effective study sessions.

- **Why**—Have a goal for each study session. The goal shouldn't be "I will make my eyeballs look at every word on these thirty-five pages," but should state what you will do in and learn from this session. Having a specific goal in mind helps you form mental expectations that are then more easily met during the study session.

In addition to the five W's of time management, seven principles of learning and time will help you build single-session study plans and thus study better.

1. **Spread out your study sessions**. It is easiest to remember what you learn first and last on a list. Therefore, if you can increase the number of "firsts and lasts," you can increase your effectiveness. In practical terms this means that you will learn significantly more in four 1-hour study blocks than in one 4-hour study block. Change subjects approximately every half hour to hour. Vary study demands and activities to have as much variety as possible. Study sessions should be scheduled accordingly. Right-brain-dominant students especially need a variety of tasks throughout their days and study sessions.

2. **Make time for review**. The first time you are exposed to material is very important, but review time is equally important. A successful study schedule has built-in review time.

3. **Set deadlines**. If you plan to "study until you are done," you may never finish. Therefore set an ending time for projects. Deadlines also serve as a motivator—if you begin the project you will know it will end.

4. **Build a buffer zone**. Plan buffer zones to finish tasks. If you decide you will need exactly 15 minutes to work each math problem, you will experience a great deal of tension if you give yourself exactly 2 hours to do eight problems. If you allot an extra 15 or 20 minutes in the study session (not per problem), you will have less stress if you run into a snag.

5. **Take regular breaks**. Breaks are important for both the mind and the body. Include 5- to 10-minute breaks every hour. Right-brain-dominant students tend to prefer study sessions with frequent short breaks while many left-brain-dominants prefer longer sessions with less frequent but longer breaks. Since few of us can watch TV for only 5 or 10 minutes, it is probably *not* a good idea to turn on the TV for breaks. A quick walk, stretch, or other brief diversion should be enough to rejuvenate you. The pacing and rhythm of study sessions is very individualized. What is your ideal pacing? Set your study plans accordingly.

USING THE SINGLE-SESSION STUDY PLANNER

It is important to write down goals for study sessions so you can monitor your progress. Applying the time management principles described in this chapter, fill out the single-session study planner shown in Figure 3.10 *before* you start studying.

Group activity: Discuss your filled-out single-session study planners in a group. Compare and contrast your ideas with other group members'. What can you learn from them? What can they learn from you? How can you all improve your time management skills?

6. **Give yourself rewards**. Rewarding yourself for finishing the session is an enticement to finish. Don't make the reward one you would give yourself regardless of whether you finish, but related to finishing and reaching your goals. In addition, choose rewards that are good for your body and wallet. You shouldn't eat a dozen chocolate chip cookies or buy a new outfit every time you finish reading one chapter. One cookie per chapter would be more appropriate.

7. **Cluster ideas**. See how ideas from similar classes relate to one another. Take time to focus on the big picture.

PROCRASTINATION

If time management means self-management with regard to time, then procrastination is a classic case of self-mismanagement. *Procrastination* here means needlessly delaying a task to the point of experiencing discomfort. Most students procrastinate some of the time, and many become chronic procrastinators. Why? Why do we choose to make ourselves so uncomfortable and anxiety-ridden?

People mismanage time for many reasons. Some do it to *gain attention*. If you are the last to arrive while a group of friends is waiting to go to a movie, you get a lot of attention when you finally show up. There is also *power* in procrastinating. If a group has to wait to start a meeting until one person arrives, that late arriver has a great deal of power over the group. Many procrastinators do so to *avoid the unpleasant*—they put off tasks they dislike. Others are *afraid of failing*. If they wait until the last minute, they can blame their poor grade on procrastination rather than failing at the task itself. The converse is also true: Some students are *afraid of success*. They worry about the added pressures, expectations, and responsibilities that come with success, so they procrastinate in order to avoid the bur-

Time you Plan to Start and Stop[a]	Subject You Plan to Study—and How Much You Can Accomplish Realistically	Actual Time You Started and Stopped (check off as completed, and comment on the quality of the session—what worked? what didn't work?)

[a]Correlate time with your optimal concentration span in this subject.

Figure 3.10
Single-Session Study Planner

den of success. Many students are simply *overloaded*. They have taken on too much, haven't prioritized their goals, and can't see the light at the end of the tunnel, so they quit trying at all. Some procrastinators are *perfectionists*. They procrastinate because they want to do everything perfectly—and if there isn't enough time for a perfect performance, they never start. Many students procrastinate because there is a kind of thrill involved. A professor friend of ours will drive down the street with his gas gauge reading empty. He will have money in his wallet and time to stop for gas, but he'll pass multiple gas stations just to see how far he can get before he runs out of gas. This is known as "riding on excitement." Many students wait until the last minute because only when the pressure is really on them can they get motivated to do the work.

How do you deal with procrastination? First, you need to become aware of your self-destructive behavior. If our professor friend never actually runs out of gas, it isn't a problem. But if he waits too long and is late for work or social events, then it becomes a problem. The same is true for schoolwork. If a student procrastinates and is able to turn in an "A" paper or earn a perfect test grade, then no real harm has been done. But if the performance is less than ideal, the student needs to treat procrastination as a problem. Many students procrastinate until their performance is compromised. They know they could have done better if they had retyped the paper, printed it out one more time, run it through the spell checker program, or had a friend or tutor look it over. If time is the reason they didn't do these things, then they need to do something about it.

Once you become aware of your self-destructive behavior, you can make plans to stop procrastination. This involves, first, answering the following questions. You may wish to write these in your journal or talk them over with a counselor or teacher.

- Why do I procrastinate? What are the causes?
- When do I procrastinate? Is there a specific time of day? If so, when is it?
- Do I procrastinate only with certain tasks? Is it hardest for me to start the task, to keep going with it, or to finish it?
- What are the "rewards" of my procrastination? What benefits do I get from doing it?
- What are the "costs" of my procrastination? How is it hurting me and those I care about and/or are responsible for?
- Whom do I procrastinate with? Who causes me to procrastinate and to drop all the things I should be doing and go to the movies? Is this person really helping me reach my goals? How much time do I spend allowing this person to influence me?
- What are my avoidance tactics? What perfectly reasonable activities do I perform at an unnecessary time to put off doing something else I should be doing—for example, cleaning out closets, drawers, garages, or an entire apartment; eating; reading the newspaper; taking a nap so I can "really be alert"; returning phone calls; or writing long overdue letters?

EXERCISE 3.6

DEALING WITH PROCRASTINATION

In your journal or on a separate piece of paper, answer the questions dealing with procrastination. In a group discuss the various responses and suggest solutions. DO IT NOW!

Now that you know the why? when? what? and who? of your procrastination, you can start planning how to reduce, control, and eliminate it. Your plan needs to be based on your own answers to the previous questions; what works for one person may not work for another. Your progress will be gradual. At first you should try to reduce how much you procrastinate. Then you can try to control it. Finally you can work at eliminating the self-destructive behavior. This can be done by taking the following four steps:

1. **Set a goal**. Make this a specific, measurable, observable goal, such as "I will do my reading before I watch TV." Don't set too many goals at once. Write down your goal in your calendar or journal. Writing it down makes it real and gives you a better chance of making it happen. It is important to develop a belief in the possibility of attaining your goals.

2. **Check your progress**. Take note of all the times you achieve your goal. Remember the gold stars our elementary school teachers put on charts when we were good? Give yourself some gold stars—either literally or mentally.

3. **Get support**. Have a friend, roommate, parent, child, or spouse help you reach your goals, and report your progress to this person regularly. Enlist these people to be your own private cheering squad.

4. **Give yourself rewards**. Make these rewards healthy for your body and checkbook. And whether psychological or material, make them real enough to motivate yourself, and award them only when you have reached your goal. Knowing there is a light at the end of the tunnel or a prize at the end of a fight well fought can be a real motivator.

Managing time and study is a real challenge for students. Using the skills presented in this chapter, you will be able to experience a sense of being in control of your life. This is a vital skill that, once mastered, will set you on the path to college success.

Notes

[1]The concept of prime internal and prime external times is from Alan Lakein, *How to Get Control of Your Time and Your Life* (New York: Signet, Penguin, 1973).

4

RECOGNIZING DISCIPLINE INFORMATION PATTERNS

Tips

1. Use information sorters to select and organize basic information.
2. Pay attention to what your instructor or textbook author stresses at the beginning of a new topic to help yourself organize information.
3. Follow the data collection patterns appropriate to different subjects as you begin learning more and more about each subject.
4. Apply basic information sorters for specific subjects to organize information in a meaningful way.
5. Use academic learning patterns to examine the structure and overall pattern of a subject as well as to make sense of specific details.

A Left-Brained Overview

I. Basic Information Sorters
   A. What they are
   B. How to create them
II. Commonly Used Information Patterns
   A. Simple list
   B. Chronological or sequential list
   C. Comparison and contrast chart
   D. Cause and effect patterns
III. Information Sorters for Specific Subjects
   A. Art history
   B. Foreign languages
   C. History
   D. Literature
   E. Math
   F. Science

A Right-Brained Overview

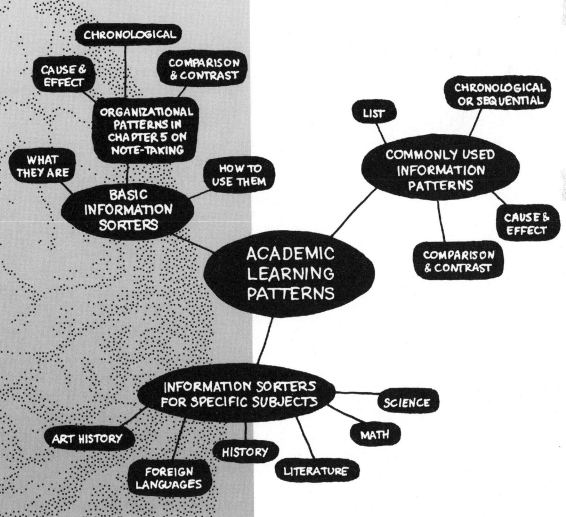

You've just started classes and you're confused. You don't know where to begin to learn about these new subjects. You're not sure what's important and what can wait until later, and you don't know how to figure it all out. In this chapter we'll introduce you to some basic information sorters to guide you through the maze of ideas and facts in your new courses. We'll also give you tips on how to apply these information sorters to specific academic disciplines.

IS THIS YOU?

BASIC INFORMATION SORTERS

These sorters can be used with any subject to collect basic, initially relevant information. Figure 4.1 shows a sorter that can be used when you are learning about a person; Figure 4.2 shows a sorter that can be used when you are learning about an event. The questions in these two sorters can serve as very specific main idea labels for your lecture notes. The answers to these questions can give you a foundation on which to build additional knowledge as you learn more about the subject.

COMMONLY USED INFORMATION PATTERNS

Knowledge of commonly used prose organizational patterns for presenting information will allow you to select, relate, and

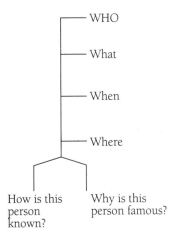

Figure 4.1

Information Sorter for Collecting Information About a Person

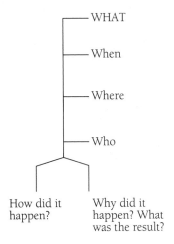

Figure 4.2

Information Sorter for Collecting Information About an Event

organize the main ideas and supporting points of a lecture or text more quickly. If you are aware of the organizational structure the lecturer or author is using, you can look and listen for the relevant points. These organizational patterns also give you alternate ways of writing down lecture information and taking notes from your texts. Common patterns include the simple list, the chronological or sequential list, comparison and contrast, and cause and effect.

Simple Lists

Typical information organized in this pattern includes names, dates, types of things—for example, types of phobias, respiratory illnesses, or poisonous reptiles—and characteristics or

EXERCISE 4.1

USING INFORMATION SORTERS

Using Figure 4.1 or 4.2 as a model, select pertinent information from one of your textbooks or class-rooms about a person or event. Try to record the information visually—that is, in chart form.

examples of a topic—for example, characteristics of a small-business purchasing analysis or examples of nonverbal behavior. Introductory phrases that signal simple lists include the following:

Advantages of	Parts of
Benefits of	Problems of
Disadvantages of	Purposes of
Examples of	Types of
Kinds of	Uses of

A typical simple-list idea cluster might look like this:

English Language Time Periods
    Old English—mid-5th century–1100 AD
    Middle English—1100–1500 AD
    Modern English—1500 on

Chronological or Sequential Lists

Typical information organized in this pattern includes dates or events being discussed in the order of their happening—for example, the events leading up to the Boston Tea Party or to the discovery of penicillin, or the steps taken to track down a criminal as written by your favorite mystery writer. In addition, process or "how-to" information—such as how to dissect a frog, create a flow chart, or prepare a speech—is usually given in this organizational form. Introductory phrases that signal chronological or sequential lists include the following:

History of	Methods of
How to	Steps in process of

Figure 4.3 shows a sample chronological list.

> Invaders Who Influenced English Language Development
>
> 597—St. Augustine and 39 missionaries introduced habit of extended writing
> • England became scholarship center
> • Bede wrote <u>Ecclesiastical History of England</u>
> • most writing in Latin
> 787—Scandinavian raiders invaded north
> 850—Raiders began permanent settlements
> • Destroyed what they couldn't use; example=books

Figure 4.3
Sample Chronological List

Development Points	Subjects being Compared	
	FREUD	JUNG
PARTS OF PERSONALITY	Id, ego, and superego	Added: Personal (cultural archetypes) unconscious and racial unconscious
DEVELOPMENTAL STAGES	Oral, anal, phallic, latency, and genital	Believed in lifelong developmental stages
HOW PROBLEMS DEVELOP	Conflict between conscious and unconscious sexual desires; fixation at developmental stage	Individual out of balance as a result of pressures; not in charge of self and own future or fate

Figure 4.4
Sample Comparison and Contrast Chart[1]

Comparison and Contrast

Typical information organized in this pattern includes the similarities among and differences between two or more related items—such as the plays of Shakespeare and Jonson, the personality theories of Freud and Jung, or mercantilist versus laissez-faire economic systems—and a subject examined both before and after a specific event—for example, the American economy and work force before and after World War II. Introductory phrases that signal comparison and contrast include the following:

Comparisons to   Differences between

Contrasts between   Similarities among

Figure 4.4 shows a sample comparison and contrast list.

Cause and Effect

Typical information organized in this pattern includes the causes or results of historical events, psychological disorders, biological functions, sociological behaviors, scientific processes, and physiological functions. Introductory phrases that signal cause and effect include the following:

Causes of   Results of

Effects of   Reasons for

Events leading to

This organizational format is displayed in one of two ways, depending on whether you are showing one cause with several

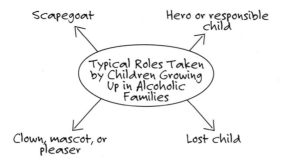

Figure 4.5
Sample Cause and Effect Chart Showing One Cause and Several Effects[2]

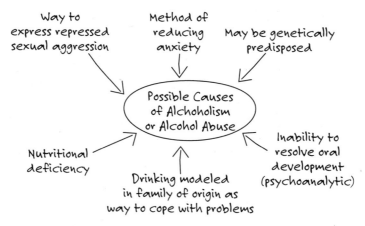

Figure 4.6
Sample Cause and Effect Chart Showing Several Causes and One Effect

results (see Figure 4.5) or one result with several causes (see Figure 4.6). In each figure the direction of the arrows shows which event came first and then led to subsequent events.

TIPS FOR STUDYING SPECIFIC SUBJECTS

Each subject or academic discipline has its own thought patterns, structure, and vocabulary. Following are some ideas on how to master studying in specific subject disciplines.

Art History

The key to remembering specific pictures or images in highly visual subjects is first to categorize the picture and then to list the characteristics of its group. For example, you might classify Giotto's *Madonna and Child* as one of several Italian early-Renaissance paintings of Christ and Mary. Any painting of the Madonna and child of this period will have common elements such as the child seated on Mary's left side and Mary

APPLYING INFORMATION PATTERNS

In either a lecture or a textbook, locate a chunk of information organized in one of the patterns described here. Select the relevant information and write main points and supporting details in the format shown. Once you've determined the organizational pattern, pay attention to what clues tip you off to the presentation of another supporting point.

Note: You may choose to do this in groups and either share the organizational patterns you've found or read them to the other members of your group so they can practice taking organizational pattern notes.

Tip: These formats are excellent ways to organize your ideas for writing.

usually dressed in blue with her head tilted toward the child. By learning these general characteristics and then picking out one very distinctive feature from the specific piece of art you are trying to remember, you will help jog your memory for that work. In the case of Giotto, the Madonna's robe has a wide, heavy gold edging down the front. Using the group characteristics of Italian early-Renaissance Madonna-and-child painting and combining it with the heavy gold edging on the Madonna's robe should trigger your remembering Giotto's *Madonna and Child*. What you are doing is using the memory principle of *selectivity* by focusing on one very distinctive feature instead of trying to take in all the individual details.

Foreign Languages

Learning a foreign language requires working on visual, auditory, and kinesthetic levels. You need to learn to understand the language when someone speaks it to you as well as be able to speak yourself. You need to learn to recognize the written words when reading and to write them yourself. Many foreign language classes start you reading and writing before you've learned to speak the language, which runs counter to the way you learned your first language or languages—understanding the spoken language, speaking yourself, and then reading and finally writing.

In addition to following the methods and assignments of your foreign language class, you can do several things to increase your language skills at all three levels—speaking, reading, and writing.[3] The first step is to set general learning objectives:

1. Learn vocabulary, especially the names of everyday objects.
2. Learn four to five basic verbs and their conjugations (present, past, and future tenses).
3. Learn the basic structure or syntax of statements and questions.

Next, you should practice speaking, reading, and writing by doing the following:

1. Learn vocabulary by naming things aloud that you see every day.
2. Learn vocabulary, syntax, and reading skills by reading in the language. *Suggestion:* Check out children's books written in the language from the library; these are more likely to be at your language level. Progress to reading things you like in the language. Many college libraries have newspapers, *Reader's Digest*, and novels in a variety of foreign languages.
3. Listen to tapes in the language; many children's books have tapes.
4. Learn to *think in* rather than mentally *translate* the language.
5. Play games that involve understanding the spoken language and moving the body.
6. Look for other ways to use the language as you go about your everyday activities.

As you develop skill in the language, try to do the following:

1. Learn more difficult or less common verb forms.
2. Learn irregular verbs.
3. Practice writing paragraphs, using simple sentences.
4. Practice speaking the language.
5. Learn basic grammatical rules by practicing them.
6. Listen to the spoken language—movies, TV programs, songs, tapes of novels, plays, and so on.

Important tip: Because language builds on itself, it is *vital* to study language every day. Three hours of intensive study on the weekend will not produce the same results as studying the language for an hour daily. Ideally, practice your language skills in many short study sessions repeatedly throughout each day.

History

With a subject such as history, it is tempting to jump into a pool of details and begin learning small bits and pieces of information. Although you do need to learn names, dates, and events, your prime task should be to organize such data into related groupings in order to understand their significance and the cause and effect interrelationships of a series of historical events. Figure 4.7 shows a chart you can use to select and sort information about a single historical event. Then you can link several related events to understand the bigger picture.

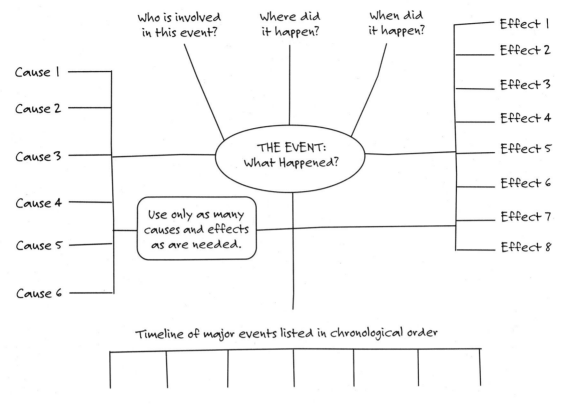

Figure 4.7
Information Sorter for History

Literature

When reading any work of literature or viewing a film, you can use the chart shown in Figure 4.8 to create a foundation of information about the work. With this information in hand, you will be ready to do a more in-depth analysis.

Math

First, you must learn basic definitions and symbols. Reserve several pages at the beginning or end of your math notebook to record math symbols and to list terms for which you need precise definitions.

If you are rusty in doing basic mathematical functions, purchase or check out a lower-level math textbook, or buy a study aid such as the laminated $8\frac{1}{2} \times 11$ pages containing all the basic facts for a subject. These are designed to be carried in your notebook for quick, easy reference.

In class take lecture notes in which you record examples showing how the instructor did a problem. Write explanations of the steps in the margin.

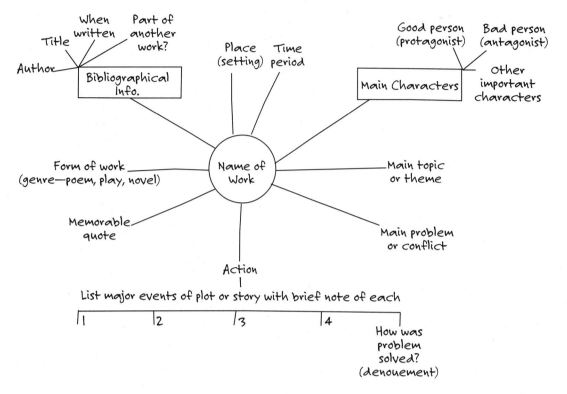

Figure 4.8
Information Sorter for Literature

Important tip: Because mathematical knowledge builds on itself, it is *vital* to study math every day. Three hours of intensive study on the weekend will not produce the same results as studying math for an hour daily. Ideally, practice your math skills every day during your PIT—that is, when you are most alert.

Science

Precise terminology and definitions are especially important in scientific disciplines. A good way to learn basic terminology is to apply the **fact-intensive topic sentence (FITS) formula**. As you encounter key terms and definitions, record them on 3 × 5 notecards. Then use the cards to group related terms and concepts, paving the way to an understanding of underlying scientific processes. (Chapter 6 explains FITS in more detail.)

As you become more familiar with how to study specific disciplines, you will begin to train your mind to automatically sort information in various disciplines. This will enable you to see how the disciplines fit together and are interconnected. This is the essence of higher education.

**APPLYING INFORMATION SORTERS
IN SPECIFIC DISCIPLINES**

In one or more of your classes, choose a subject information sorter that fits a chunk of information you need to learn about and understand. Use the sorter to guide you in selecting the most relevant information and in organizing that information visually and kinesthetically. If you are auditory, recite the information aloud as you collect and organize it.

Notes

[1]Information about the personality theories of Sigmund Freud and Karl Jung taken from James Kalat, *Introduction to Psychology*, 2nd ed. (Belmont, CA: Wadsworth, 1990), pp. 471–79.

[2]Information about typical roles of children raised in an alcoholic home taken from Claudia Black, *It Will Never Happen to Me* (New York: Ballantine Books, 1981); Janet Woititz, *Adult Children of Alcoholics* (Pompano Beach, FL: Health Communications, 1983); and Joy Miller and Marianne Ripper, *Following the Yellow Brick Road* (Deerfield Beach, FL: Health Communications, 1988).

[3]For a detailed language-learning plan that incorporates right- and left-brain techniques as well as various senses, see Sheila Ostrander and Lynn Schroeder, *Superlearning* (New York: Delacorte Press, 1980).

5

TAKING LECTURE NOTES

Tips

1. Decide why you are taking notes, what information you want, and how much detail you need.
2. Learn and use one basic note-taking format, and develop variations of that basic format to fit requirements of different classes.
3. Write lecture notes in series of idea clusters.
4. Record only essential main ideas and key supporting details, in your own words and in legible handwriting.
5. Develop your own set of abbreviations and symbols for faster note-taking.
6. Within 24 hours after taking notes, revise and finish them by correcting any errors, adding omitted information, clarifying unclear points and abbreviations, and highlighting main ideas.
7. Review lecture notes regularly.

A Left-Brained Overview

A Right-Brained Overview

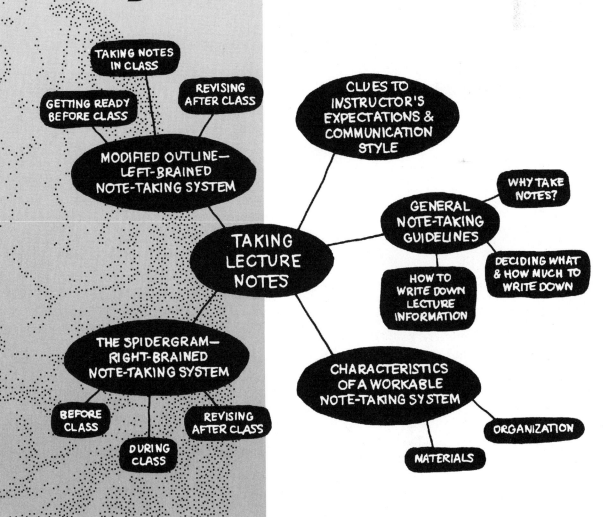

TAKING NOTES IN CLASS

GETTING READY BEFORE CLASS

REVISING AFTER CLASS

MODIFIED OUTLINE— LEFT-BRAINED NOTE-TAKING SYSTEM

CLUES TO INSTRUCTOR'S EXPECTATIONS & COMMUNICATION STYLE

WHY TAKE NOTES?

GENERAL NOTE-TAKING GUIDELINES

DECIDING WHAT & HOW MUCH TO WRITE DOWN

TAKING LECTURE NOTES

HOW TO WRITE DOWN LECTURE INFORMATION

THE SPIDERGRAM— RIGHT-BRAINED NOTE-TAKING SYSTEM

CHARACTERISTICS OF A WORKABLE NOTE-TAKING SYSTEM

BEFORE CLASS

DURING CLASS

REVISING AFTER CLASS

ORGANIZATION

MATERIALS

You're looking over your notes from one of your lecture courses, and you realize you're in trouble. You tried to write down everything your instructor said, but now all you have is several pages of alien scribble. In this chapter we'll give you a system for taking comprehensive—and comprehensible—notes in your lecture courses. In fact, we'll give you two systems, one left-brained and one right-brained, so that you can adapt a system that works best for you in all your courses.

IS THIS YOU?

CLUES TO YOUR INSTRUCTOR'S EXPECTATIONS AND COMMUNICATION STYLE

Before you can take effective lecture notes, you need to understand your instructor's expectations and communication style. This means paying close attention to his or her comments about what the class will cover, what assignments you'll have, how the course grade will be calculated, and what policies govern late papers. It also means attending to the instructor's nonverbal communication behaviors such as physical gestures and facial expressions. Paying attention to a lecturer's nonverbals is a good way to get a sense of what that person is like as well as what he or she thinks is important. Look for these common nonverbal communication behaviors:

ATTENDING TO NONVERBAL COMMUNICATION

Pay close attention to one of your instructors. Notice what typical nonverbals she or he uses to emphasize important lecture points. Then, try to discover one or two of her or his individual nonverbals that signal, "This is important." Make sure you take notes on all information signaled by the nonverbal behaviors. You may want to code it so you'll remember that it was stressed nonverbally. This information will guide you in later study so you concentrate on points the instructor considers important.

- Making eye contact with the students
- Lowering the tone of the voice
- Speaking slower and enunciating words more carefully
- Glancing at notes to make sure he or she has the information correct
- Making some physical gesture to emphasize a point
- Writing on the chalkboard or using an overhead projector
- Distributing information on handouts

Spoken information accompanied by these behaviors usually means that the instructor is signaling important information. Code this information in your lecture notes because there's a good chance it'll be a test question.

GENERAL NOTE-TAKING GUIDELINES

Why Take Notes?

Active note-taking is a powerful way to begin learning new material. It turns a passive learning environment into a participatory one. Taking clear, detailed, and organized lecture notes is an excellent way to "study," to save precious time using classtime both to record new information and to begin learning it, and to create thorough, well-organized materials for future study. Moreover, it gives strong clues to potential test questions.

What and How Much Should You Write Down?

At the beginning of the semester, answer these questions for yourself in order to plan your note-taking strategy in each class:

- How much of the lecture information is repeated in the textbook?

- What type of test or demonstration of knowledge will be required in the class?
- Is this an introductory class or a subject new to me?
- How much do I want to know about the subject?

Availability of lecture information Understanding the basic structure of a class's lecture is one way to decide how much and what to write in lecture notes. During the first two or three weeks, compare the content and organization of the lecture with that of assigned reading material. Many college lecturers can be categorized into one of these three groups, which will give you guidelines about what type of notes to take in that class.

- **Textbook repeaters**. These instructors go over the main points of the assigned readings but add little in the way of new information. You should probably take notes on the main points mentioned in class. However, you may find it workable to highlight the main points in your textbook instead of taking formal written lecture notes.
- **Half-and-half lecturers**. These instructors review major points from the assigned readings and add new information during lecture. Not only should you record or highlight the main points repeated from the text, but be sure to take detailed notes on the new material.
- **Just-new-stuff lecturers**. These instructors do not go over assigned readings and do not repeat information given in the textbook. Instead, they shower you with lots of new information. In such classes you need to take extensive and detailed notes. First, concentrate on main ideas and key supporting details. Then, record as many other details as possible.

Demonstration of knowledge The majority of college classes check your learning in a subject with a test. Therefore it's important to find out early in the semester what type of test will be given since different types of tests require students to concentrate differently on different parts of the course material. Knowing what type of test you'll have helps you decide on the type of information to include in your notes.

Objective tests—multiple choice, true-false, matching, and fill ins—ask questions about major subject concepts and specific facts given in either the lecture or the textbook. Thus they require a lot of memorization of facts as well as an understanding of broad, general concepts. Lecture notes for a class with objective tests need to include both the main points and the supporting details. Record names, dates, and places mentioned by the lecturer since you will be held accountable for these on the test.

Essay or subjective tests require you to demonstrate your knowledge and understanding of major concepts. But to do this you must also know details. In such a class, concentrate on taking notes that help you understand and explain the major concepts. Focus first on the major ideas and then use the facts to clarify or support them. In essay tests you do not always have to cite the same supporting points mentioned in the lecture, but you must demonstrate your knowledge and understanding by including some supporting details and specific facts.

Application tests require you to show your understanding of a subject by demonstrating your ability to apply your knowledge. Math, science, foreign languages, accounting, computer science, and English composition are some classes that typically give application tests. In these classes take notes on how you solve a specific problem or perform a process. Include all the steps and be very specific and detailed. Then, learn how to do it; don't just memorize it.

Introductory class or new subject Such classes always require you to learn basic concepts, subject vocabulary, and new ways of thinking about information. Because you are usually unfamiliar with all these basics, the class seems hard. Concentrate on becoming familiar with the subject's vocabulary, procedures, and basic facts. You'll probably need to take a lot of notes.

Level of knowledge desired Realistically not every college class will hold the same amount of interest for you. For some classes you may only want to learn about the subject, earn a reasonable grade, and move on. In other classes, such as ones in your major, you'll probably want to learn and remember as much as possible. We aren't advocating that you just blow off a class that's not your prime interest. But we must point out that it's natural to be more interested in one subject than another. Take adequate notes in all classes, but take more in-depth notes in classes that interest you more.

How Should You Write Down Lecture Information?

Instructors lecture a lot, and deciding what to write down can be difficult. Some students try to solve this problem by writing everything down. If that were the answer, we could simply tell you to buy a good tape recorder and tape every lecture. Good note-takers do not record everything said. What, then, should you write down?

EXERCISE 5.2

ADAPTING YOUR NOTE-TAKING TO SPECIFIC CLASSES

Use the questions discussed previously to analyze the lectures in one or more of your classes. Decide what type of information to write in your lecture notes to meet the learning requirements for that class. Write the analysis or discuss it with a group.

Good notes capture the important points and supporting details that help you understand the general subject and remember the lecture information. As a note-taker your primary job is to evaluate the ideas presented in the lecture and organize your notes to show the relationship between facts and ideas. That's easy enough to say, but if you are new to college, how do you do it? How do you know what's important when everything the instructor says sounds important?

Focusing on the "big picture" Think of a class lecture as a jigsaw puzzle. A lecture is usually about one subject, just as a jigsaw puzzle has one picture. However, both lectures and puzzles have a lot of small pieces that combine to form the whole picture. Rather than trying to put together a puzzle by randomly fitting pieces together, many people begin by sorting pieces into related groups—pieces of sky, pieces of trees, pieces of a house, and so on. When taking lecture notes, you need to do the same type of sorting in order to get an idea of what different idea groupings the lecture might contain. This is easier to do with some lecturers than others. (This organizational approach is also extremely useful in making sense of textbook readings. See Chapter 6, "Reading College Textbooks," for a full discussion of the sorting process.)

Some lecturers will begin class by stating what points they will talk about. Others will write a brief outline on the chalkboard. In these cases your job as note-taker is to record the main points and listen for and write down supporting or clarifying details for each main point. With this type of lecture, we suggest that you begin each class's lecture notes by recording the main topics to be covered. That way you have an overview, and if the lecturer doesn't have time to cover something, you have a record of what she or he intended. Sometimes instructors forget they didn't lecture on a topic they intended to and ask exam questions about it.

Other lecturers don't tell you what points they'll focus on. In these cases you have to figure out the main points as you go along or even after the lecture is over. Generally instructors assume that you have the background information because you have been assigned related reading prior to the lecture. Therefore failing to read before class is equivalent to having the lecture outline on a chalkboard that everyone but you can see. It's important to familiarize yourself with assigned readings before the lecture, whether by reading every word of the chapter or simply previewing it.

Taking notes in idea clusters No matter how organized or unorganized, most lecturers talk in terms of relationships. Thus, your task is to take notes in "idea clusters." Each idea cluster has two basic parts—the name or title for the information in the cluster and the supporting details. First, write the cluster name, being as detailed and specific as possible. Use the four W's of journalism to help yourself do this:

Who is being discussed? Name the individual or group of people.

What subject is the information about?

When did the subject take place? Write down the year, century, or time period.

Where did the subject take place? Name the city, state, or country.

Figure 5.1 shows a sample idea cluster about one aspect of the history of the English language.[1] Notice how many of the four-W fact questions have been answered in this idea cluster's main idea label:

WHAT **WHO** **WHERE**
<u>Invasions</u> Brought <u>New People</u> to <u>England</u>

An idea cluster gives you questions to answer by listening for information in the lecture. Such questions also help you select important supporting information to write in your notes.

The lecturer may talk in more detail about one or more of the four-W fact questions. Look at the supporting details in Figure 5.1 recorded for this idea cluster label. The note-taker

Invasions Brought New People to England

- Angles
  - settled in N. 2/3 of island
  - called land Anglaland
- Saxons
  - settled in S. 1/3 of island
- Jutes
  - settled in Kent, Hampshire, Isle of Wight
- Took 3 tribes 150 yrs. to gain control of all of Eng.

Figure 5.1
Sample Idea Cluster

CREATING IDEA CLUSTERS

Practice selecting the four-W facts to create an idea cluster label from a lecture or textbook, or practice this skill when listening to TV and radio programs. Then, choose points or details that support the topic. Do this by reading a paragraph or section and creating the idea cluster label with supporting details, or have someone read to you while you create the idea cluster label.

has written information to answer the questions Who came to England? and Where did they settle? Other parts of the lecture will probably discuss more about the invasions.

After stating the main idea, lecturers typically discuss this idea in one of three ways. To help yourself decide what's important enough to write down, use Laia Hanau's PIE mnemonic as a listening guide:[2]

Proofs to explain or support the conclusion

Information about the idea cluster subject

Examples to explain or clarify the idea cluster topic

The idea cluster is like the individual puzzle piece. When you put enough of the pieces together, you get the whole picture.

CHARACTERISTICS OF A WORKABLE NOTE-TAKING SYSTEM

To help yourself remember the qualities of effective notes, use the NOTES mnemonic:

Neat—If you can't read the notes later, they are useless. Make them neat.

Organized—If the information isn't written in an easily understood form, the information will be much harder or impossible to learn.

Terse—If you write too much stuff down, you'll be overwhelmed by it all. Be selective; write in brief phrases; use abbreviations.

Efficient—No matter how good a system is, if it takes too much effort and time, most people won't stick with it. Use a system that is easy to follow and does not take large amounts of time to complete.

Sense—To be worth anything, the information you write down must make sense many weeks later. Therefore, be detailed, specific, precise, and concrete. Organize as you go. Ask questions if you don't understand. When in doubt, write down more, rather than less information.

Before you can take good notes, you need the right tools. First, get yourself some $8\frac{1}{2} \times 11$ notebooks, spiral or loose-leaf. Next, create a designated place for class handouts in your notebook. Finally, get some pens with waterproof ink, preferably blue or black. Pencil smears; felt-tips are sometimes hard to read and blur when wet; colors can be difficult to read or highlight.

Now that you're familiar with the basic qualities of effective notes and the tools needed to create those notes, you're ready for some specific tips:

1. Begin each new set of daily notes on a new sheet of paper.
2. Record class assignments in one place. One option is to reserve several pages in the front of the notebook; another is to always leave a few lines at the top of the first page of the day's notes. In either case be sure to transfer assignments to your master schedule and weekly organizer (see Chapter 3 on time management).
3. Use idea clusters to write lecture information in a graphic display form that shows the relationship between main ideas and supporting details.
4. If you know the lecturer is switching topics, skip one or two lines between each idea cluster.
5. Write notes in words and phrases, not complete sentences or paragraphs.
6. Use standard abbreviations to make note-taking faster.
7. Write notes in your own words. This begins the process of transferring information to your memory.
8. Emphasize vocabulary of the subject in your notes. You may choose to code such terms in your notes. If a class lecture has lots of subject vocabulary, you may find writing subject vocabulary on 3×5 note-cards rather than in your notebook a useful technique. (See Chapter 6: "Reading College Textbooks," for an effective way to handle learning vocabulary terms.)
9. Develop a set of note-taking codes to help you quickly identify important items in your notes—for example, *T* for possible test question, *V* for vocabulary term, and *?* for something you have a question about.

THE MODIFIED OUTLINE—
A LEFT-BRAIN NOTE-TAKING SYSTEM

This classic note-taking system uses a modified outline format and has space for potential study questions and notes to yourself. Among its strengths is that the process of taking and completing the notes forces you to review frequently and produces notes ready to be studied, while already beginning to store the information in your memory. And it is useful in all types of classes.

Getting Ready Before Class

1. **Set up the note and question columns**. On a new sheet of paper draw a line for the question column approximately 2 inches from the left edge. Left-handed note-takers may prefer to reverse the format by placing the wider note column on the left and the thinner review column on the right. Figure 5.2 illustrates the two-column set-up.

Questions	Notes
	Space for lecture summary (optional)

Figure 5.2
Note Paper Set-Up for Left-Brain/Modified-Outline Note-taking

PRACTICING WITH IDEA CLUSTERS

With a group of classmates, practice taking notes in idea clusters. After class take turns reading or presenting information to each other.

Alternative activity: Listen to recorded speeches or television documentaries or news programs and take notes in idea clusters.

2. **Get ready to take notes**. Write the class name or code, lecture date, and page number in the top right-hand corner. On the first page of the day's notes, list the lecture's main topic. Figure 5.3 shows an example.

3. **Review the previous lecture's notes**. Spending a couple minutes skimming these notes serves both as a minireview and as a warmup for the day's lecture. Doing this before each class will help you learn the course material a bit at a time.

Tip: Try previewing any reading assignments or making a preview spidergram (see the next section and Chapter 6, "Reading College Textbooks"). Bring it to a class as a lecture guide.

Taking Notes During Class

Take notes in idea clusters. Be sure to use an easy-to-read display format. Figure 5.4 shows an example of notes from part of a lecture on the history of the English language.

Revising Notes After Class

1. **Revise your notes within the first 24 hours after taking them**. Research shows that the most forgetting occurs during the first 24 hours after first coming into contact with information.

2. **Quickly reread your notes**. In particular check for the following:
   - *Omissions*. Correct these by adding the missing information. If revision is done soon enough, you'll be able

		ENG 150	Class name
		10/22/98	Date of lecture
		Early history of	Primary topic
		Eng. Language	of lecture
		p.1/	Page number

Figure 5.3
Example of Organizational Information in the Top Right-hand Corner of Lecture Notes

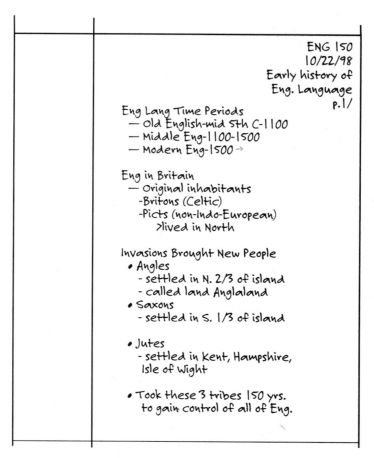

Figure 5.4
Sample Left-Brain/Modified-Outline Notes

to remember most of the information. If you can't remember, put a question mark in the margin to remind yourself to ask the instructor or another student in class.

- *Incorrect information.* Correct it or check the textbook, talk with your class note-taking buddy, or code it as a question to ask the instructor at the next class or during office hours.
- *Abbreviations.* Make sure they are understandable. If not, write them out.

3. **Highlight main ideas**. You can either underline, box, or highlight with a colored marker. Do this to distinguish main ideas from supporting points.

4. **Write study cues in the key-word column**. Options for doing this include the following:
   - Writing words or phrases to cue your memory about information in your notes.

- Writing test questions in the margin or on 3 × 5 note-cards. Note that writing test questions in the same format as your tests will help you become familiar with how the lecture information will be transformed into exam questions. This makes tests less mysterious and scary, as well as allowing you to focus on learning the information rather than worrying about the test. Be aware, however, that objective test questions take a lot of time to write, so do only two or three objective questions for each set of lecture notes.

5. **Summarize your notes**. Options include the following:
   - At the end of a set of lecture notes, write a short paragraph summarizing the important points of that day's lecture. This is a powerful way to begin storing the information in your memory as well as a useful review tool.
   - Make a mnemonic and write it on a 3 × 5 notecard or at the top of the page where the information is located. Mnemonics are effective information retrievers. (Chapter 7, "Using Memorization Techniques," gives examples of mnemonics and information on how to create them.)
   - At the end of your notes, you may find it helpful to write your own thoughts, ideas, and reactions to the lecture. This technique is particularly useful in classes such as philosophy that require you to develop your own conclusions.

6. **Study and review your notes**. Figure 5.5 shows an example of revised lecture notes from Figure 5.4. To review them, cover up the note column and study the material by recalling answers to the study questions.

EXERCISE 5.5

TAKING LEFT-BRAIN/MODIFIED-OUTLINE NOTES

For one lecture period in one of your classes, take notes in the left-brain/modified-outline form. After class, revise your notes. Compare your notes with our examples. Make any needed changes. Then, take left-brain/modified-outline notes in a class for at least two weeks. It will take that long to learn and feel comfortable with a new note-taking system.

Group activity: Get together with other class members to compare and review notes. By reading and discussing each other's notes, each of you can create a more complete set of notes while making sure you understand the main points of the lecture.

ENG 150
10/22/98
Early history of
Eng. Language
p.1/

3 Stages of Lang Dev & their times	**Eng Lang Time Periods** — Old English-mid 5th C-1100 — Middle Eng-1100-1500 — Modern Eng-1500 →
All the following were early inhabitants of Eng except A. Angles & Jutes B. Britons, Picts & Jutes C. Angles, Saxons & Jutes D. Angles, Jutes & Celts	**Eng in Britain** — Original inhabitants -Britons (Celtic) -Picts (non-Indo-European) >lived in North ———————Settlers **Invasions Brought New People** • Angles England - settled in N. 2/3 of island - called land Anglaland • Saxons Eng - settled in S. 1/3 of island
Describe where the 3 invading tribes settled	• Jutes - settled in Kent, Hampshire, Isle of ~~Wright~~ Wight • Took these 3 tribes 150 yrs. to gain control of all of Eng.

Write a summary of the lecture here or write reminders of important terms to learn or information about upcoming assignments or tests

Figure 5.5
Sample Revised Left-Brain/Modified-Outline Lecture Notes

THE SPIDERGRAM—A RIGHT-BRAIN NOTE-TAKING SYSTEM

Although the spidergram format may look strange to you, the information it contains is the same as that found in the left-brain/modified-outline format. It is just placed differently on the page. **Spidergrams** are useful in classes where the lecturer jumps from topic to topic, for students who are very visual, and in classes that stress visual information or require that a lot of information be synthesized. Spidergrams are also a great way to select and organize the main ideas and supporting points from a textbook chapter. Students who are right-brained or visual may find spidergrams very much to their liking. However you feel about them when you first see them, give them a try. You may be surprised at the results.

Getting Ready Before Class

1. Consider using a sketchbook larger than your regular $8\frac{1}{2} \times 11$ notebook.
2. Try turning your notebook or sketchbook sideways so that the pages are wider than they are long.
3. In the top right-hand corner, identify the notes you are about to take, just as you would with the left-brain/ modified-outline system. Include the same information shown in Figure 5.3.

Taking Notes During Class

1. Draw a circle in the center of the page and write the main lecture topic inside the circle.
2. Branch out from the center, writing one main idea at the end of each branch line.
3. Add supporting details to the main idea branches. Figure 5.6 shows an example of spidergram lecture notes containing some of the information in Figure 5.4.
4. Carry a pack of 3×5 cards with you to class. Use these to write down vocabulary terms and their definitions. You may need to write the term on the card during class and finish the definitions outside of class. This will keep the spidergram notes from being too cluttered and will provide you with a set of personal flashcards to learn the important terms for that class. (Chapter 6, "Reading College Textbooks," provides a technique for making vocabulary notecards.) These terms/definitions

EXERCISE 5.6

TAKING RIGHT-BRAIN/SPIDERGRAM NOTES

Try outlining a textbook chapter using the spidergram method. After you are comfortable with spidergrams, you may want to take spidergram lecture notes in some of your classes.

Group activity: Use the spidergram format to review a lecture or a concept by having different members of your study group add another piece of the information. The group participation and discussion plus the visual format will help you review the information differently from the way that you originally learned it. (Reviewing in ways different from the original learning is an effective learning technique.)

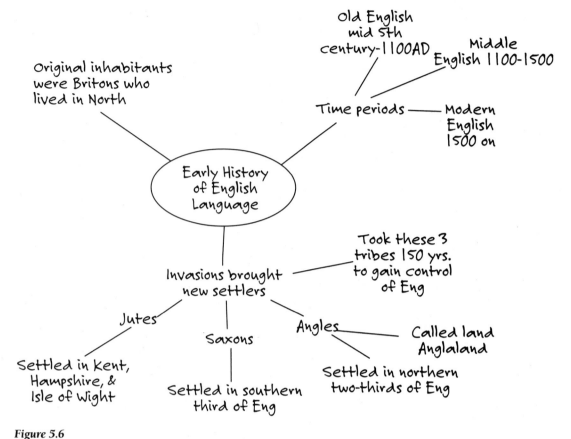

Figure 5.6
Sample Right-Brain/Spidergram Notes

can also be written in the form of minispidergrams if you prefer.

Revising Notes After Class
1. Follow the guidelines for revision given in the left-brain note-taking section.
2. Try highlighting the various levels of the spidergram notes with different colors so that the lecture topic is highlighted in one color, the main ideas in another color, and the supporting details in a third color. If juggling all these colors drives you crazy, however, don't do it.
3. Write study questions either at the bottom of the note page or on 3 × 5 notecards. If you use notecards, code them with class and lecture date.

Give spidergrams a try. Many students are surprised at how much they like the method once they get comfortable with it.

Rather than trying to learn it while taking notes in a lecture, begin by taking spidergram notes from a textbook chapter. Once learned, the method can be used during a lecture, either for the entire lecture or as part of a left-brained note format.

Notes

[1]Information about the early history and development of the English language from L. M. Myers, *The Roots of Modern English* (Boston: Little, Brown, 1968), Chapter 4.

[2]PIE mnemonic from Laia Hanau, *The Study Game: How to Play and Win with "Statement Pie"* (1974).

6 Reading College Textbooks

Tips

1. At the beginning of the semester, preview all your textbooks so you'll know what is in them.
2. Find the typical pattern of your texts so that you can predict where the major points are located.
3. Figure out how your assigned reading relates to the lectures and tests.
4. Adapt your reading to your preferred learning style (visual, auditory, kinesthetic, left- or right-brained, and so on).
5. Schedule the length of reading sessions to match your high-quality concentration time.
6. Preview each chapter before reading, highlight the main ideas while reading, and then review the chapter.
7. Schedule regular review sessions.
8. Focus on new vocabulary.

A Left-Brained Overview

A Right-Brained Overview

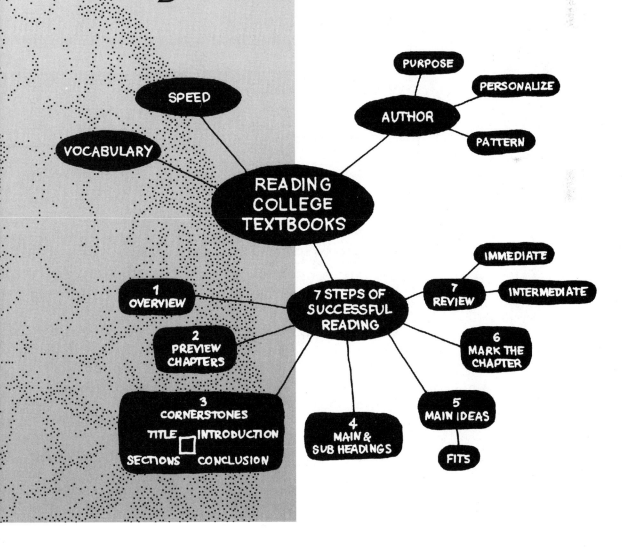

You're having some problems reading your college texts. You find it difficult to pick out the information from your reading that will be on your tests. And you're having trouble remembering what you have read. If so, you may suffer from a very common student "disease" known as "eyeball separatis and detachis." In this condition you know your eyeballs are looking at the words on the pages, but somehow your eyes feel separated and detached from your head—nothing is going in your head or sticking there. In this chapter we will show you the cure to this dreaded malady and help you master college reading.

IS THIS YOU?

DISCOVERING THE AUTHOR'S PURPOSE AND PATTERNS, AND PERSONALIZING THE TEXT

If you think of your textbooks as jigsaw puzzles, you can put together the meaning of the chapters. It is important to note that a puzzle begins as one whole picture or giant piece, which is then cut into individual pieces and boxed. Similarly authors do not randomly fill pages with words to make a book (although this may sometimes seem to be the case). Rather, authors have a *purpose* in writing each section, each paragraph, and even each sentence. Once you can determine why the author is presenting the information, it becomes easier to determine what the main ideas are and how they relate to the other ideas in the chapter. Discovering the author's purpose is the first stage in curing eyeball separatis and detachis. Using the puzzle analogy, discovering the author's purpose is akin to deciding which puzzle to buy.

Authors also write in certain *patterns* that give important clues to the reader. Most authors follow the same pattern throughout each chapter in the text. Most sections and paragraphs also follow similar patterns. As a reader your job is to determine what the pattern is and use the pattern in studying the textbook. For example, an author might begin each paragraph with an introductory sentence and then a thesis statement that contains the main idea of the paragraph. This thesis is followed by supporting details, a conclusion, and then a transition to another paragraph, which repeats the same pattern. Some authors put the main idea at the end of each paragraph; others put it in the middle. Some start with examples; others end with examples. The wise reader will focus on the writing patterns as well as the information given and thus will learn to spot where the main ideas are stated.

In addition to learning to identify authors' purpose and pattern, you need to own or *personalize* your reading—that is, to get personally involved in your reading. By personalizing your reading, you internalize it so that it "belongs" to you. Tony Buzan in *Use Both Sides of Your Brain* calls this the organic study method.[1] In the organic study method, learning takes place from the individual out, not from the subject matter in. When information is personalized it is easier to understand and remember. Personalizing the text is akin to purchasing the puzzle: You buy it, take it home, and begin to work on it.[2]

SEVEN STEPS OF SUCCESSFUL COLLEGE READING

Once you have brought home your newly purchased puzzle, it is time to begin working on it. Once you have purchased the required texts for your classes, it is time to begin working at making sense of them so you can both learn and perform well on examinations. The following seven-step process will enable you to do just that.

1. **Overview the text**. This is the same as looking at the picture on the box. From overviewing the text, you will begin to see what the "puzzle" will be about.

2. **Preview each chapter**. This is equivalent to dumping out all the pieces and turning them over. It is vital to preview before reading each chapter so that you will begin to see what the "puzzle" consists of.

3. **Examine chapter cornerstones**. This is analogous to finding the four corner pieces. Chapter cornerstones include the chapter title, chapter introduction, chapter sections, and chapter conclusion.

4. **Focus on chapter headings**. This is akin to finding the edge pieces. These main and sub-headings give the chapter its shape and boundaries and tell where the ideas will go.

5. **Sort the main ideas from details**. The main objects in the puzzle are similar to the main ideas in the chapter. Just as there are background "sky" pieces in the puzzle, there is background information in the chapters as well. Your task is to sort the background from the main ideas as you actually read.

6. **Mark up the chapters**. This is equivalent to finishing the puzzle by putting every piece in place. Only by highlighting, underlining, and making notes on or in the chapter can you ensure full comprehension.

7. **Review**. Stop and admire the puzzle when it is done.

Let's examine each of these steps in the reading process in more detail.

1. Overviewing the Text

It is much more difficult to solve a puzzle without first seeing the picture of it. In the same way, it is hard to make sense of a textbook without understanding the author's purpose and goals. A way to determine the author's purpose is to overview the text before starting to read it. Be sure you know what the title of the text is. Read the author's name and see what you can learn about the author by reading the dedication, preface and introduction, and book jacket. Carefully study the table of contents. Note the name of each chapter. Ask yourself why you think the author put the chapters in that particular order. Evaluate each chapter's contents. Which chapters look interesting? Which look challenging?

Often students view their textbooks as threats. Perceived threats often cause people to tense up or freeze up. This tensing and freezing before reading inhibits the reader from understanding the material read. One good way to make the text less threatening is to overview the material in the book.

EXERCISE 6.1

OVERVIEWING YOUR TEXTBOOKS

Overview all your assigned textbooks, including this one, as described here.

Alternative activity: In the margin of the table of contents for all your texts, put a star by the two chapters that look most interesting. Put an **X** next to the two chapters that look most challenging. Doing this will get you personally involved in learning from your textbooks.

Overviewing a textbook generally takes no more than 5 minutes. And if you skip those 5 minutes, you will be hindering your ability to understand what you read. Imagine trying to watch a play without scenery, costumes, or props, and you can see the value of overviewing texts.

2. Previewing Each Chapter

Previewing the chapters is an essential step in the reading process. Chapter previewing is the same as dumping out all the puzzle pieces from the box and turning them over. The puzzle solver who skips this step often finds that the *one* piece being searched for—often the one needed to complete a portion of the puzzle or join two parts together—is the one that is not turned over. You must preview each chapter before reading it so that you can see what direction the chapter will take.

Previewing the chapter can be accomplished in many ways. Two excellent ways for right-brain and visually oriented students to preview a chapter are (1) to make a spidergram of the chapter (see Chapter 5, "Taking Lecture Notes") using only the main topics in the chapter and (2) to put the table of contents into a hierarchy of ideas. Both of these can be accomplished by focusing on the main section headings in the chapters (see steps 3 and 4 below). An excellent way for left-brain students to preview is to group all the main headings into outline form. Both right- and left-brain students also need to look at the chapter illustrations, charts, tables, and the like, as well as read the review questions at the end of each chapter, as part of the previewing process. Auditory learners will want to recite *out loud* the material that is being previewed.

Previewing should take no more than about 5 minutes per chapter. However, these 5 minutes are analogous to the 5 minutes it takes to grab a paddle before heading off in a canoe—failure to grab the paddle will leave you with no way to steer or return to shore. Failure to preview a chapter will leave you without any direction in reading or any way to connect new material to other material.

EXERCISE 6.2

PREVIEWING CHAPTERS

Practice previewing a chapter from one of your texts by making an outline and/or a spidergram of the chapter *before you read it*. Make it a habit to do this for all the chapters of all your texts.

3. Examining Chapter Cornerstones

The four corner pieces of a puzzle are gems for the puzzle solver to find. These four pieces form the foundation of or framework for the rest of the puzzle. Think of each of the four as road signs on an interstate highway. If you ignore or misread a road sign, you may end up in the wrong town or even state. Similarly, if you ignore or misread one of the chapter road signs, you may miss out on the entire direction and content of the chapter.

The first cornerstone or road sign is the *chapter title*. Reading the chapter title is an important way for you to discover the author's purpose in writing the chapter. The chapter title is like a sign saying "This Way North." If you want to go north you will follow the sign; if you want to go south you will turn around. But if you ignore the sign you will not know where you are headed. You will be lost.

The second cornerstone or road sign is the *chapter introduction*. The introduction is like a mental map or diagram that guides you a few miles down the road. The introduction should be read carefully and highlighted or marked (step 6 discusses highlighting or marking a text). Do *not* continue to read past the chapter introduction without understanding its purpose and content.

The third cornerstone or road sign is the *section headings*. These section headings are like directional signs that inform the driver of speed limits, road conditions, and the like. Think of each of these section headings as a question that will be answered in the text that follows. A successful right-brain technique is to highlight each section heading before reading the chapter. A successful left-brain technique is to convert the section headings into questions in the margins of the text or on a separate piece of paper. In either case your goal is to read in such a way that the questions are answered.

The fourth and final cornerstone or road sign is the *chapter conclusion*. The conclusion restates the main themes of the chapter and wraps up the information. The conclusion is like the

EXERCISE 6.3

IDENTIFYING CHAPTER CORNERSTONES

Highlight the chapter title, introduction, section headings, and conclusion of this chapter. Make it a habit to do this for all the chapters of all your texts; you will reach the destination of understanding much more quickly.

Alternative activity: Make questions out of each section heading in this chapter. Write the questions in your notes or in the margins of the text. Make it a habit to do this for all the chapters of all your texts.

exit sign that states your destination. It is important to carefully read the chapter conclusion before reading the chapter. This will let you know where you will be heading and when you are approaching your destination, so you don't drive right on by.

4. Focusing on Chapter Headings

The *main headings* and *subheadings* are like the edge pieces of the puzzle. They give the chapter its boundaries and tell where and how far the ideas will go, how ideas relate to one another, and where transitions occur. Like the edge pieces, the headings are essential to comprehending the "big picture." If you focus on all the chapter headings you will be able to comprehend the text in each section. The "questions" technique recommended for the section headings is applicable to the subheadings as well. Much as a detective gathers clues to solve a mystery, the successful reader studies all the headings to understand the material in the text.

5. Sorting Main Ideas from Details

Identifying your preferred reading style Only after steps 1–4 are completed are you ready to actually read a text chapter. Reading is a complex process of decoding letters and symbols to form words and to make sense of the words on the page. (*Note:* If you have problems decoding words, you may benefit from a visit to a reading clinic. Consult your school's learning assistance center to see what resources are available.)

Although decoding words is an important start, it is only the first step in college reading. For successful college reading you need to create a reading system that will help you learn information and pass tests. It is important that your reading style match your learning style. For example, right-brain, visual readers benefit from underlining and taking notes during reading. They also benefit from using new color to add details to their preview spidergrams and from drawing pictures in the margins of the text. Kinesthetic learners learn well by creating an indexing system for their texts using Post-Its while reading. (This is also an effective technique for preparing for a take-home or open-book test.) They also learn well by making 3 × 5 notecards of material to be learned and by underlining or highlighting while reading. Some kinesthetic learners learn even better if they are eating while reading (but make it a healthy brain food like vegetables or fruit, not high-sugar or high-fat junk food). Auditory learners benefit from reading the assigned material out loud. They also learn well by tape recording the main points of the chapter and chapter summaries.

EXERCISE 6.4

TURNING HEADINGS INTO QUESTIONS

Turn each heading in this chapter into a question. Write the questions in your notes or in the margins. Make a spidergram of the headings. Highlight them. Make it a habit to do this for all the chapters of all your texts.

FINDING YOUR OPTIMAL READING STYLE

Try the various reading methods listed above to identify your preferred reading style. Experiment with some of the other methods to see how they work for you.

Using the fact-intensive topic sentence (FITS) formula Sorting main ideas from chapter details is similar to sorting the central objects in the puzzle from the background pieces. The main objects in the puzzle are the main ideas in the chapter. Just as there are background "sky" and "land" pieces in the puzzle, there is background information in the chapter as well. While you are reading you must sort the background from the main ideas.

Sorting out what is important in the chapter can seem daunting to the first-time college reader, who may assume that authors hide the main ideas. However, knowing the basic terms and concepts of a particular discipline, and determining what you need to know about them, is the crucial first step in subject area learning. And all texts give clues to what the main ideas are. The clues can be found using the **fact-intensive topic sentence (FITS) formula**, which guides you in locating key information and recording it in a clear, succinct format. Applying the FITS formula will help you create idea clusters when taking lecture notes and highlight important information when reading textbooks. In addition, the FITS formula can help you do the following:

1. Learn terms in a particular discipline.
2. Learn formulas in science and math.
3. Write identification or short-essay test answers.
4. Write thesis statements for papers.

The FITS formula tells you how to *define* the idea or term being presented. In order to define the term, you must first separate the important or main information from the background by applying the FITS formula:

*definition = item name + group or category name +
3 distinguishing characteristics, functions, or uses that answer
the questions who? what? when? where? why? and how?*

For example, how do you define *banana*? In your head you know what a banana is, but how do you define it? A poor definition would be the following:

A banana is a yummy thing I had for breakfast.

This statement may be true, but it tells little about what a banana actually is. If you add the category or group name, the definition takes this form:

A banana is a yummy fruit I had for breakfast.

This is a little better, but it still doesn't state what a banana is. But what happens when we add three distinguishing characteristics to our definition?

[item name] *banana* +
[group or category name] *tropical fruit* + [3 dist. chars.]
(1) crescent shaped, (2) high in potassium, (3) yellow when ripe but gets brown when old

Therefore:

A banana is a tropical fruit that is crescent shaped and high in potassium, and that is yellow when ripe but gets brown when old.

This formula can be used to define any term, person, or concept you may encounter in any class or textbook. For example, suppose you're studying Sigmund Freud in your psychology class. How do you figure out what you need to know about Freud from the reading and lectures? If you were to ask a classmate to define Freud, this is what you might hear:

Sigmund Freud was a very important person. He studied sick people and helped a lot of them. He wrote lots of books and developed a lot of ideas that are used today even though some people disagree with some of them. He helped people understand more about how people think and act.

Although this definition contains no factual errors, most instructors would give it a failing grade! Everything in the definition is true, but it doesn't give any information specific to Freud. In fact, this definition could apply to anyone who was important and wrote books.

A better way to figure out what you need to know about Freud is to apply the FITS formula:

[item name] *Sigmund Freud* +
[group or cat. name] *doctor* + [3 dist. chars.]
19th-century Austrian theorist + [3 dist. chars.]
(1) considered the father of psychoanalysis, (2) introduced the idea of an "unconscious," (3) known for labeling the "psychosexual stages of development"

Therefore:

Sigmund Freud was a nineteenth-century Austrian doctor who was known as the father of psychoanalysis. He introduced the idea of an unconscious and is known for labeling the psychosexual stages of development.

Let's assume you happen to remember that Freud was from Vienna. Do you state this? Yes. It is best to be as specific as possible and still be correct. However, if you're not sure whether he was from Austria or Hungary, don't guess Hungary and be wrong. Rather, be more general—for example, say "eastern Europe" instead.

The FITS formula has other applications as well. For instance, if you anticipated an essay test question on Freud, you would simply expand on each point. If you were assigned to write a paper on Freud, you could write a paragraph or section on each point. If you were taking lecture notes, you would check to see whether you had answered the who, what, when, where, why, and picked out three distinguishing characteristics for each term or concept.

FITS formulas can be written in two ways: as a left-brained sentence and as a right-brained minispidergram. Suppose your art history class was studying Judy Chicago. By applying the FITS formula you might come up with this information:

[item name] *Judy Chicago* +
[group or cat. name] *artist* + [3 dist. chars.]
20th-century American feminist artist + [3 dist. chars.]
*(1) considered a feminist artist, (2) known for incorporating such
handicrafts as sewing, macramé, and quilting into her art,
(3) known for the "Dinner Party," a scene depicting various
roles of women.*

The following definition of Judy Chicago is in a left-brained format; Figure 6.1 shows the same information in a minispidergram.

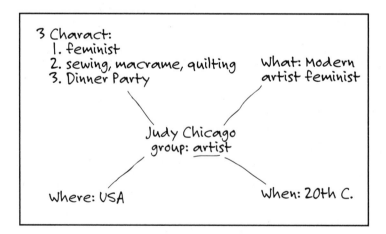

Figure 6.1
Judy Chicago Defined in a Right-Brained Format

USING THE FITS FORMULA

Practice writing FITS formula notecards for new terms and concepts you encounter in your reading and lectures.

Judy Chicago is a twentieth-century American feminist artist who sculpts and incorporates such handicrafts as sewing, macramé, and quilting into her art. She is known for the "Dinner Party," a scene depicting various roles of women.

The FITS formula is useful for learning terms and concepts as well. For example, in biology you could use the FITS formula to learn about photosynthesis:

[item name] *photosynthesis* +
[group or cat. name] *biological process* +
[3 dist. chars.] *plants, convert sunlight energy to chemical energy, shows interdependency among organisms* + [3 dist. chars.]
(1) consists of two sets of reactions, (2) light-dependent—sunlight converted to ATP & NADPH, (3) light-independent—sugars and other compounds assembled with help of ATP & NADPH

Photosynthesis defined in a left-brained format would look like the following; Figure 6.2 shows the same information in a mini-spidergram.

Photosynthesis is a biological process that converts sunlight energy into chemical energy. It consists of two sets of reactions: light-dependent, in which sunlight is converted to ATP & NADPH, and light-independent, in which sugars and other compounds are assembled with help of ATP & NADPH.

The FITS formula also works well as a study aid. As you encounter terms and concepts and ideas in your reading and

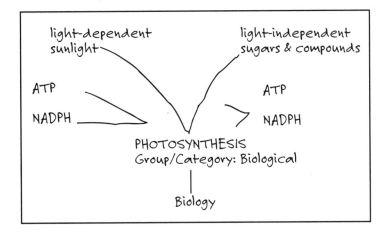

Figure 6.2
Photosynthesis Defined in a Right-Brained Format

lectures, use the FITS formula to create definitions on 3 × 5 notecards. These cards can then be used for study and review.

6. Marking the Chapter

Highlighting, underlining, and making notes on or in a chapter is called "marking" the chapter. Marking is a valuable technique by which you signal to yourself what material must be noted and learned. Among its many benefits, marking texts keeps you physically active while you are learning, keeps you focused, and helps you concentrate.

It's important that you be selective in marking. Only the most relevant ideas should be marked. Ideally you should mark about 15–25 percent of a page of text. If you mark or highlight every word on every page, there will be no signals for learning. Conversely, if you mark or highlight only three or four words on each page, there has been no sorting of main ideas from details.

You can choose from a number of systems for marking texts. Some students like to highlight texts with a felt-tip pen, while others prefer to underline with a pencil. Some students like to jot notes in the margins of the texts, while others prefer to take notes on a separate piece of paper. Right-brain students make right-brain notes such as spidergrams on the notebook paper, while left-brain dominants write the same information in outline form. Figure 6.3 shows a sample marked text featuring underlining and brief margin notes.

Is there one right way to mark a text? No! Your task is to experiment until you discover what works best for you. However, there are some basic guidelines to follow when marking a text:

1. **Read with your pencil, pen, or highlighter on the table**. When you finish reading a paragraph, section, or page of text, reflect on what you have read. Then, and only then, pick up your pencil, pen, or highlighter and mark the main points. These markings should answer the questions you posed as you read the headings and/or provide the basis for answers to potential test questions.

2. **Think first, and then mark, underline, or highlight one word or phrase at a time**. *Never* underline or rewrite whole sentences at a time. Doing so indicates that your brain has switched to "auto-pilot." Before you know it you'll be marking entire pages but not *thinking* about what you are marking.

3. **Monitor your marking to see how much marking works best for you**. Remember the suggested guideline of marking about 15–25 percent of a text. If you mark more than that, you are not sorting out the main ideas

COORDINATE SYSTEMS. Once an object has been defined in terms of its vertex coordinates in two dimensions and the object has been transformaed according to translation, rotation, and scaling matrices, then the job of the graphics package is to display the object on the output device in the correct location. Two types of

[margin note: V]

coordinate systems are used to specify and draw an object. World coordinates are the coordinates used to define the object in its original master form. World coordinates can be in meters, feet, miles, micrometers—in fact, whatever coordinate system satisfies a particular application. If the designer is designing an airplane,

[margin note: Ex.]

the coordinates may be in terms of meters or millimeters. If the designer is working on a VSLI chip, the dimensions may be in micrometers. A good computer-aided design system allows the user to design in world coordinates suitable for a particular application. The software then translates to screen coordinates to draw a picture of the object on the screen.

The second set of coordinates are called device coordinates. Device coordi-

[margin note: Vocab]

nates may be in terms of inches on a pen plotter, electrostatic plotting points on an electrostatic plotter, or even pixels on a CRT screen. The user should not need to know the particular device coordinates being used. The software typically translates the world coordinates to appropriate device coordinates specified by the user or automatically adjusted to fit on the device. Any design should be able to be drawn or defined in terms of world coordinates appropriate for the application.

These two coordinate systems define two frames of reference. World coordi-

[margin note: Uses of WORLD COORDINATES]

nates can be used to define a *window* or frame through which the user looks to see the world. This window can be thought of as being similar to an empty picture frame which can be held up to view the world. By moving the frame around, different portions of the world can be viewed. The coordinates of the corner points of the window can be defined in world coordinates because the window exists in the world, not on the screen itself (Figure 3.22).

[margin note: Uses of DEVICE COORDS]

Device coordinates can be used to define a *viewport* or frame on the device in which the view will be drawn. The viewport appears on the screen or on the output device itself. The corner points of the viewport, which is usually rectangular, are defined in terms of the device or screen coordinates. That is, the corner points may be defined in terms of pixels on a CRT, or inches on a pen plotter.

The *window* dimensions and location determine the portion of the scene seen by the observer. The location and dimensions of the *viewport* determine the location on the screen where the picture is to be drawn. Recently, the term *windows* has been applied to certain programs which display information in different regions on the screen. For example, the Apple Macintosh uses the concept of "windows" to display pull-down menus and various applications programs or pictures on the screen. For example, the Apple Macintosh uses the concept of pictures on the screen as shown in Figure 3.6. Technically, these "windows" are really viewports on the screen. Windows, remember, are defined in the world and viewports are defined on the screen.

Source: From *Computer Integrated Design and Manufacturing* by Bedworth et al., © 1991 McGraw-Hill, Inc. Used by permission.

Figure 6.3
Sample Marked Text

---

from subordinate ones. If you mark less than that, you may not be getting the main ideas.

4. **Be consistent in your marking system from class to class and text to text**.

5. **Develop your own codes or symbols**. Right-brain students tend to prefer color coding, such as main ideas

highlighted in pink, subordinate ideas in yellow, and test questions in orange. Left-brain students tend to prefer symbols, such as underlining new vocabulary once and potential test questions twice, circling answers to the questions posed in the headings, and using exclamation points, brackets, and parentheses to isolate various kinds of main ideas. Kinesthetic students often make flash cards, while auditory learners make review tapes that they can listen to later. Try each of these and create the combination that works best for you.

7. Reviewing

Reviewing the chapter is similar to admiring the finished puzzle. Unfortunately many students omit this crucial step. They read the last word on the last page of the chapter and slam the book shut. The next time they open the book is to start the next chapter. And they review all the chapters read the night before the test, but not sooner. Approaching reading in this manner causes many learning problems for students. These problems can be solved using two techniques: (1) immediate reviewing, which involves putting the bits and pieces of information together into some order that makes sense, and (2) intermediate reviewing, which involves rehearsing the bits and pieces learned so they are committed to memory.

Immediate reviewing Like overviewing and previewing, *immediate reviewing* of a chapter should take no more than 5 or 10 minutes. Nevertheless, much of the significant learning of the material takes place during this immediate review session. Here you look back over the chapter you have just read and check to see if the marking makes sense. Next you review the questions you formed during the chapter preview and the review of all headings. Has each question been adequately answered in your mind during the reading of the text? Finally you pause to reflect on and summarize the chapter. Summarizing and reflecting are vital in learning. It is reflection—thinking about what you have read—that helps you personalize and internalize the information. From this internalizing process, you can understand the author's goal and purpose. And from this understanding comes both learning and improved test performance. Once you have reflected on the material, write a one- or two-paragraph summary of the chapter, in the book itself, in your notes, or on a 3 × 5 card. Auditory learners may choose to tape the summary instead of writing it.

Intermediate reviewing With this technique you look back over all the material at an intermediate time between when the material was first read and the night before the test.

Many students schedule regular time for intermediate reviewing at the end of each week. Think about a backpack full of supplies for a hiking trip. Without the backpack of essentials, the hiker would need to return to home base each night to obtain new supplies. With the backpack, however, the hiker can make significant progress away from the home base. Intermediate reviewing resembles that backpack in that it enables you to carry information learned in reading with you through the semester. Intermediate reviewing is a way of keeping the information learned during reading sessions fresh in your mind. It helps overcome forgetting and eliminate the need for cramming. It allows learning to take place as you go over the material to be learned a number of different times. To use intermediate reviewing successfully, the time allotted for the sessions will continuously increase from the first week of the semester until the last. Review time is vital for success, especially in classes with comprehensive examinations.

Tips for Reviewing

1. **Review using your preferred learning style**. For example, visual learners can review by creating a hierarchy of a single chapter or several chapters, making pictorial summaries in margins or on Post-Its, or highlighting spidergrams or notes made while reading. Kinesthetic learners can review by walking or using a stair climber or exercise bike while reviewing flash cards or notes or spidergrams made during reading. They can also create an imaginary spidergram or hierarchy on the floor or ground, stepping to the position on the floor or ground that represents the point they are reviewing and reciting out loud the material learned. Or they can color in their spidergrams and outlines with different colors or sort their vocabulary cards into a hierarchy or spidergram on the floor or table. Auditory learners can review by reciting out loud the material to be learned and by playing back tape recordings of chapter summaries, vocabulary cards, and/or reading notes.

2. **Make spidergrams (right-brained) or outlines (left-brained) of the material being reviewed**. You can also make master spidergrams or master outlines that link and combine all the individual chapter spidergrams and outlines. This is an excellent way to show the relationships between the ideas in the whole textbook.

3. **Create potential test questions for each chapter studied**. Visual learners can do this by drawing a line down the middle of a piece of notebook paper and writing the questions on one side and the answers and text page number on the other and then quizzing themselves. Kinesthetic learners can do this by listing the questions on 3 × 5 cards, with the answer and text page number on the flip side of the card. They

can then review the stack sorting the cards into piles of known questions, unknown questions, and questions about which they are unsure. (Chapter 9, "Taking Objective Tests," discusses test preparation and test-taking in detail.) Auditory learners will benefit the most from tape recording these questions. No matter what your preferred style, review the whole set of test questions at each intermediate review session.

4. **Recite the material to be learned out loud**. Reciting is the fastest way to get information into the brain. Reciting is a powerful learning tool because all three learning channels are activated at once in what is called *synergistic learning*. Synergistic learning takes place during reciting because you use the visual channel when looking at the material, the auditory channel when hearing the material, and the kinesthetic channel when reciting the material.

Ultimately your goal in reading college texts is to make the seven steps *habits*. Once you begin to do this on a regular basis, you will feel more and more comfortable. Allow yourself time to get used to trying out these new techniques, and modify them to fit your learning style until you experience success with them.

Two more areas of college reading need to be addressed: reading speed and vocabulary development.

SPEED AND READING

College students have busy lives! You want to do well in school and also have some fun. You may think you could better understand your texts if you spent more time reading them. However, deep inside you would rather spend less time hitting the books. It's a dilemma—you want to decrease the amount of time spent on reading while increasing the amount of material you learn from it. Unfortunately this goal is only partially attainable.

There are some techniques for spending less time reading while keeping retention high. However, the goal of college reading is *not* speed, it is comprehension. Often it is possible to read certain types of material, such as newspapers and novels, quite quickly, but this is not always the case for college reading. The goal of college reading is *retention*, both for overall learning and for successful test performance. Reading speed and reading comprehension can be thought of as opposite ends of a teeter-totter. The more speed goes up, the more comprehension goes down, and vice versa. Your goal is to balance speed with retention and comprehension.

To maximize reading speed while maintaining a high rate of comprehension and retention, do the following:

1. **Don't view the reading as a punishment or threat**. Instructors do not assign reading to make you suffer. If you can't figure out why you are being asked to read something, ask your instructor. Understanding the purpose of the assignment can help improve speed. Books are inanimate objects that cannot harm you. Students who perceive books as threats often freeze when reading and are unable to concentrate.

2. **Take steps to ensure successful reading**. For instance, read at a time in your awake/sleep cycle when you are most awake and alert. Also, read at a time in your eating cycle when you are neither too hungry (you won't be able to concentrate) nor too full (you will feel sleepy). In addition, read in a place that is comfortable in terms of temperature and seating—but not in bed. Finally, turn off such distractions as the TV, phone, radio, and so on. Put a sign on your door that says, "Do Not Disturb."

3. **Ignore some of the common myths about reading and speed**. For example, despite what you may have been taught, reading aloud helps both comprehension and retention. Also, it's perfectly acceptable to use a pencil or colored 3 × 5 notecard to help you keep your place in the text.

Another technique for increasing reading speed is expanding your eye movements. As children learning to read, we are taught to stop and sound out every syllable of every word, a pattern that can continue into adulthood. The best way to increase reading speed without losing comprehension is to

EXERCISE 6.7

PRACTICING SPEED READING

Practice expanding your eye movements while reading the rest of this chapter. Make it a habit to do this for all your reading.

Alternative exercise: In the beginning practice reading for 15 minutes. Then stop and check to see how many pages you covered and whether you comprehended what you were reading. If you didn't comprehend the information, stop and determine what specifically is causing the problem. Is it the level of the material? The vocabulary? Your concentration level? Remedy each problem using the suggestions in this chapter until you are comfortable reading and comprehending for 15 minutes at a time. Once you can comprehend a certain number of pages in 15 minutes, increase the number of pages you cover in the same time period. Slowly increase both the time and pages until you have maximized your ability to read quickly and retain a sufficient amount of information for success.

> (The) (dri) (ving) (for) (ces) (for) (a) (new) (des) (ign) (ap)(proach)
> (in) (clude) (both) (e) (con) (o) (my) (and) (part)
> (func) (tion) (al) (ity). (Increased) (compe) (tition) (is)
> (coming) (from) (Europe) (and) (Japan) (in) (the) (form) (of)
> (lower-cost and) (better quality) (products). (Some progress)
> (has been made) (recently in design) (improvement in the)
> (United States.)
> (The coveted Milan Golden Compass Award) (for Design was
> awarded) (in 1987 to an American company) (for its Automated
> Coagulation Laboratory), (a medical analysis) (instrument.)

Source: From *Computer Integrated Design and Manufacturing* by Bedworth et al., pp. 137–138. © 1991 McGraw-Hill, Inc. Used by permission.

Figure 6.4
A Speed Reading Experiment

lengthen the number of syllables and words you can absorb with one eye movement. To illustrate, begin reading the passage in Figure 6.4. Stop and focus your eyes on the dots above each word or set of words in the parentheses. As should be quickly evident, the more times you force your eyes to stop and fixate, the slower you read. The goal is to increase the number of phrases your eyes can absorb with one stop or fixation. Of course, if you concentrate too much on your eye movements, you won't be able to also focus on the material. The trick is to incorporate expanding your eye movements naturally and gradually.

VOCABULARY DEVELOPMENT IN COLLEGE

One of the ways instructors evaluate whether students have mastered a subject is to check students' vocabulary comprehension. Instructors want to see if students can "talk the talk." In most lower-level, survey-type college classes, the material is presented in a way that exposes you to the vocabulary of the discipline. If you increase your vocabulary, you will increase your chances of doing well in school.

Each academic discipline has its own set of vocabulary. To succeed you need to design a way to incorporate these new words into your own "internal dictionary." The wrong way to learn vocabulary is to memorize lists of words created by someone else. A better way is to keep track of new words introduced in your classes and learn them as you encounter them. To do this, try the following:

EXERCISE 6.8

BUILDING VOCAB FILES

Create a VOCAB file for all your classes. Match the VOCAB file format to your preferred learning style.

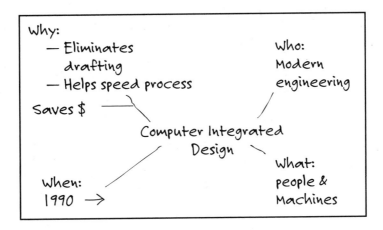

Figure 6.5
Sample Left-Brain (bottom) and Right-Brain (top) VOCAB Cards

1. Make it a specific goal to learn new words. This intention can help in accomplishing the goal.
2. In taking lecture notes, mark each new vocabulary word with some type of symbol—perhaps a box or a double underline.
3. When reading, create a similar system to designate new vocabulary in your book or in your notes.
4. Make a class VOCAB file on 3 × 5 cards. A right-brain modifications of this is to use a different color card for each class subject (all new biology terms on green cards, all new history terms on yellow cards, and so on). Figure 6.5 shows sample left- and right-brain VOCAB notecards.

Improving both reading speed/comprehension and vocabulary are proven ways for you to achieve success in higher education. These are by-products of effective study techniques and can be easily incorporated into your study sessions.

Notes

[1] Tony Buzan, *Use Both Sides of Your Brain* (New York: E. P. Dutton, 1974).
[2] Tony Buzan, *Make the Most of Your Mind* (New York: Linden Press/Simon & Schuster, 1984).

USING MEMORIZATION TECHNIQUES

Tips

1. Maintain a positive attitude and an interest in the subject you're studying.
2. Study for short periods of time on a regular basis rather than cramming.
3. Involve all your senses to enhance the memory imprint.
4. Group items to be learned into related categories rather than trying to memorize long lists of unrelated items.
5. Set specific study or learning goals for each session.
6. Study in an environment that is positive for you in terms of noise, lighting, furniture, and location.
7. Before beginning to study, set the stage for remembering by making yourself calm and relaxed.

A Left-Brained Overview

I. Mental Attitude and Memorization
  A. Check prior subject knowledge
  B. Set a goal
  C. Maintain interest in the subject

II. General Memorization Methods
  A. Association
  B. Classification
  C. Consolidation
  D. Distributed practice
  E. Recitation
  F. Selectivity

III. General Guidelines for Better Memorization
  A. Have a specific learning goal
  B. Study in a positive environment
  C. Set the stage for remembering
  D. Involve as many of your senses as possible
  E. Work with the material to be learned in several ways
  F. Overlearn material to delay the forgetting process

IV. Types of Memorization Devices
  A. General Characteristics
  B. Rhymes
  C. Mnemonics
    1. Acronyms
    2. Coined sentences
  D. Loci-based memory systems
    1. Number-rhyme auditory system
    2. Number-shape visual system

A Right-Brained Overview

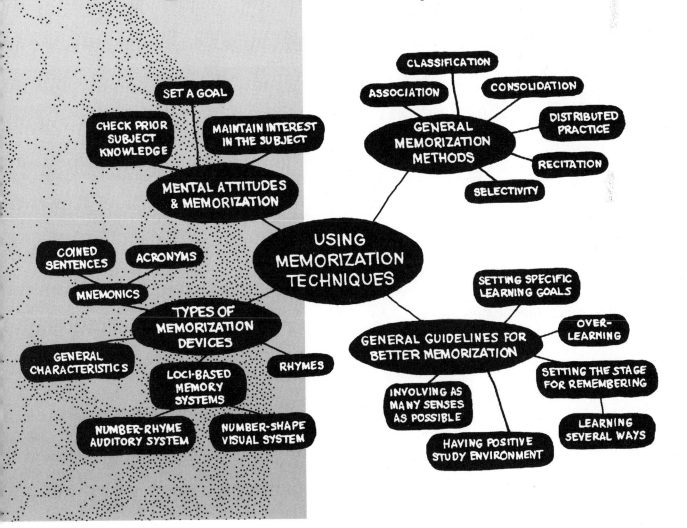

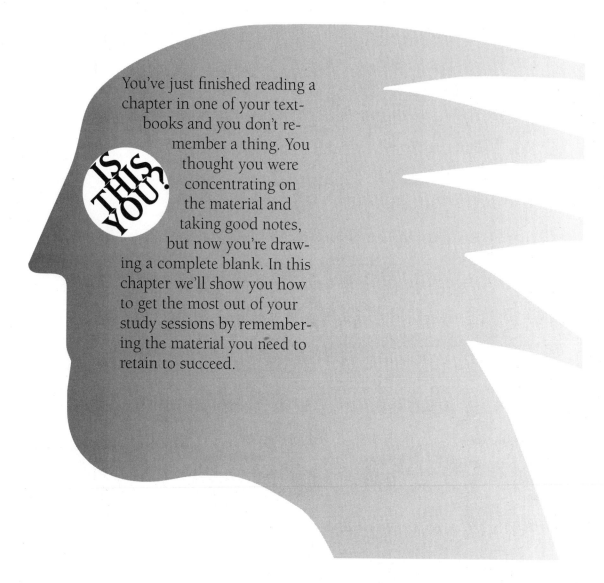

You've just finished reading a chapter in one of your textbooks and you don't remember a thing. You thought you were concentrating on the material and taking good notes, but now you're drawing a complete blank. In this chapter we'll show you how to get the most out of your study sessions by remembering the material you need to retain to succeed.

APPLYING PRINCIPLES OF MEMORIZATION

Mental Attitude and Memorization

How you think and feel about a subject affects how you learn and remember. To improve your mental attitude, and thus to enhance your memorization, do the following:

1. **Check your prior subject knowledge**. It is easier to add new knowledge to things you already know. Before beginning to work on a new subject, think about or brainstorm informal notes about what you already know about it. If the subject is brand new, relate the new things you are learning to something you are already

DEVELOPING A POSITIVE ATTITUDE

Review what you already know about a certain subject. Set a goal to remember a specific portion of the content. If you are having particular difficulty with a subject, try talking to someone who likes it to find out what interests him or her so much about the subject.

familiar with. For example, relate the chance of a gene mutating to the odds of getting a certain hand in five-card draw poker.

2. **Set specific goals**. If you have a purpose or goal in mind when working on material, it aids your remembering. When you go to class, sit down to read a chapter, or study for an exam, set specific learning goals. You might say, "I'm going to remember all the main points the instructor talks about in lecture today," or "I'm going to learn Freud's and Jung's stages of human development by the end of this study session."

3. **Maintain interest in the subject**. If you are interested in a subject, you generally learn more quickly and easily. So, search for ways to get yourself interested in each of your subjects. Realistically, this may prove difficult for some of your subjects, but, give it a try. Dig into the subject. Talk with someone who has an interest in or is knowledgeable about the subject. Their enthusiasm may rub off on you. Think of ways you'll benefit by learning this subject.

General Memorization Methods

The basic method for transferring something from short-term, temporary memory to long-term, more permanent memory involves reviewing material a number of times in short study sessions. The children's television show "Sesame Street" provides good examples of this technique. Watch the show sometime and count how many times during the hour one of the characters recites or sings or otherwise presents the ABCs or the numbers 1–20. In similar fashion, by repeatedly working with the material to be learned over a number of sessions, you can ensure retention. Try some of the memorization principles discussed below to select and organize information you need to learn in a class, and then go over it a number of times over several days or weeks. The key, ultimately, is to review, review, and review again!

- **Association**. Relate new information to familiar or known material. Apply this to your academic work by consciously trying to see how you can relate new information to something you've already learned.
- **Classification**. Organize information into related groups. Classifying material reduces how much you have

to learn by clustering similar things together, thus saving you time. Apply this by taking one of your instructor's study guides and creating several related groups of terms or concepts. Then you can code each group for faster and more efficient retrieval by using a mnemonic. (See the section in this chapter on creating mnemonics.)

- **Consolidation**. Be aware that it takes anywhere from several seconds to a few minutes for your brain to transfer information from short-term to long-term memory. Apply this principle to your studies by giving yourself time to enable new information to sink in.
- **Distributed practice**. Study in shorter periods of time spread over several days or weeks. This principle is closely related to that of consolidation. Apply this principle by creating a study schedule that allows you to work on a subject several times a week rather than in one huge block of time.
- **Recitation**. Repeat something to be learned over and over. Apply this principle in combination with distributed practice to help yourself retain material.
- **Selectivity**. Note that it is easier to remember less stuff than more. Apply this principle by reducing what you have to learn to smaller groups by classifying pieces of information into related groups.

General Guidelines for Better Memorization

In addition to using the principles of memory, follow these six guidelines:

1. **Have a specific learning goal**. Instead of just studying psychology, history, or math, create a specific learning task. For example, resolve to learn ten psychology vocabulary terms or the effects of the Vietnam War on American society. Having a specific goal makes it easier to accomplish it.
2. **Study in an environment that is positive for you**. This means sitting in a comfortable (but not too comfortable) chair and working in a well-lit, distraction-free place—no TV, loud music, music with words, or interrupting friends. (See Chapter 3, "Managing Your Time," for more details.)
3. **Set the stage for remembering**. If you are excited, worried, or upset, remembering things is harder. In fact, one of the signs of stress for some people is forgetting or losing things. Thus, before you begin studying, use a relaxation technique such as meditation or visualization to put yourself in the best frame of mind to study and remember. In addition, suggest Sheila Ostrander and Lynn

Schroeder, studying with baroque instrumental music that has a 4/4 beat playing softly can enhance learning (Vivaldi and Pachelbel are two composers whose music they recommend).[1] Ostrander and Schroeder also offer several excellent visualization exercises.

4. **Involve as many of your senses as possible**. The more senses involved in the learning, the stronger the memory imprint. Therefore, try diagramming the information to be learned (visual and kinesthetic senses) while reciting it aloud or to yourself (auditory sense). Add color to your diagrams for more impact. Experiment with different learning styles and techniques to find out what works best for you.

5. **Work with the material to be learned in several ways**. In addition to diagramming and reciting, talk the ideas through. Test yourself by answering questions, both written and aloud. Check your knowledge by using FITS VOCAB cards (see Chapter 6, "Reading College Textbooks") and practicing both seeing the term and responding with the definition, and seeing the definition and responding with the term. Explain the information to a study group.

6. **Overlearn material to delay the forgetting process**. The stronger the learning, the harder it is to forget it. So, work with the material until you know it backwards and forwards. It'll reduce the amount of forgetting that occurs.

TYPES OF MEMORIZATION DEVICES

Memorization devices are ways to organize and code chunks of information so you can retrieve them more quickly and easily from your brain. Think of memorization devices as resembling a computer file name. When you call up a file, you get whatever you stored in it. Memorization devices use the principles of memory discussed previously and provide specific steps for memorizing information.

General Characteristics

Effective memory devices might feature the following characteristics:

- **Visual**. Seeing is a strong sense. Adding a visual component to your memory device will tap into this powerful memory aid.
- **Silly or corny**. If something is funny, it helps us remember it better. It's not necessary to consciously add silliness to your memory devices, but if this quality is there, don't worry about it. It's a positive.

EXERCISE 7.2

APPLYING PRINCIPLES OF MEMORIZATION

For one of your classes in which you need to memorize some information, try one of the techniques discussed above. Did it seem to help you remember the material?

- **Risqué**. The human mind seems to remember things that are sexually suggestive. If associating material with something risqué helps you remember it, that's fine. No one else has to know *how* you're retaining material.

In addition to these characteristics of effective memory devices, you can apply elements of the various learning styles to strengthen your remembering. For example, as a visual learner, you can add a picture, a diagram, a cartoon, or a moving picture sequence to what you want to remember. Such visuals can be real or fictional pictures. As an auditory learner, you can add sound, music, or dialogue to your picture. You can create rhymes and make up songs using the information. Recite the information out loud or to yourself. As a kinesthetic learner, you can try learning information standing up or walking around. You can associate what you are learning with a physical movement such as touching each of your fingers as you list the items to be remembered.

Specific memorization devices include (1) rhymes, (2) mnemonics, and (3) loci-based systems.

Rhymes

Rhymes are one of the oldest methods for remembering. No doubt you're familiar with the rhyme for remembering how many days are in each month of the year:

Thirty days hath September,
April, June, and November.
All the rest have thirty-one,
'Cepting February, which is minus some.

Another example of a memory rhyme is this one, which summarizes the fate of Henry VIII's six wives:

Divorced, beheaded, died.
Divorced, beheaded, survived.[2]

If rhymes appeal to you, organize the facts you want to remember into rhyming lines. The number-rhyme system discussed later in this chapter can help you create rhymes.

Mnemonics

Mnemonics are retrieval codes you create from the initial letters of the information you want to remember. Think of a mnemonic as the file name under which you store your data. Of course, if you put nothing in the computer file, then you get nothing out when you open it. A mnemonic is not a substitute for knowing; it is merely a way to organize and quickly remember packages or files of information.

There are two basic types of mnemonics, depending on how you must remember the information: (1) acronyms and (2) coined sentences.

Acronyms Either real or real-looking words made up of the initial letters of each piece of information are called **acronyms**. Acronyms are useful when you do not have to remember the information in any particular order. An example of an acronym many of you learned in geography class is HOMES, which names the five Great Lakes:

Huron
Ontario
Michigan
Erie
Superior

To create an acronym, simply take the first letters from each key piece of information and fiddle about with them until you've created an actual or real-looking word. Don't worry about correct spelling. As long as the acronym is something that you can remember, use it.

Coined sentences Sentences made up of the initials of each piece of information in a given order are called **coined sentences**. Coined sentences are useful when you want to remember chunks of information in a certain order. For example, the following coined sentence helps musicians remember which notes go on the lines of the staff:

Every Good Boy Does Fine.

This mnemonic triggers the correct placement of notes on the lines beginning with the bottom line of the staff. Similarly, biology students remember the parts of the animal kingdom using the following mnemonic:

King Philip Sometimes Comes Over For Girlie Shows.

From the first letters of each word in the coined sentence, we have Kingdom, Phylum, Subphylum, Class, Order, Family, Genus, and Species. To the biology mnemonic we usually add the silly visual image of a seventeenth-century French king walking down a street of ill-repute (see Figure 7.1). This visual

TYPES OF MEMORIZATION DEVICES

CREATING MNEMONICS

Make a mnemonic for a chunk of information you want to remember precisely. When you are tested, notice if and how the retrieval device helps you to recall. Experiment with the different types to see which ones work best for you.

image helps trigger the mnemonic.

To create your own coined sentences, write the first letters of each main word or phrase and see what type of sentences you can develop. Remember, this shouldn't take you more than a minute or two. For example, to remember the order of the planets from the sun outward, first write down the initial letter of each planet in order from the sun:

M_____ V_____ E_____ M_____ J_____
S_____ U_____ N_____ P_____

Then develop a sentence to fit the letters:

My **V**ery **E**arnest **M**other **J**ust **S**erved **U**s **N**ello's **P**izza.

And this sentence helps you remember Mercury, Venus, Earth, Mars, Jupiter, Saturn, Uranus, Neptune, and Pluto.

Loci-Based Memory Systems

The loci memory system developed by the ancient Greeks is one of the oldest methods of remembering. Greek philosophers and orators would associate the points of their speeches with a portion of a room or the location of an object in a room they were very familiar with. *Loci* refers to places that the Greeks linked with the points they wanted to make in their speeches. Two memory systems related to the loci concept are (1) the

King Philip Sometimes Comes Over For Girlie Shows

Shows This Way

Figure 7.1
Visual Image to Trigger Coined Sentence for Remembering the Parts of the Animal Kingdom

number-rhyme system, which adds an auditory component, and (2) the number-shape system, which contains an additional visual element. To use either system, begin by learning a base or loci to which you'll forever after attach the items you want to remember.

Number-rhyme system   To create your own number-rhyme system, for each number from one to ten link an item that is tangible (one that actually exists physically) and that also rhymes with the number. Figure 7.2 gives some examples. These rhyming pictures will be your permanent memory foundation. To remember something in either a specific or random

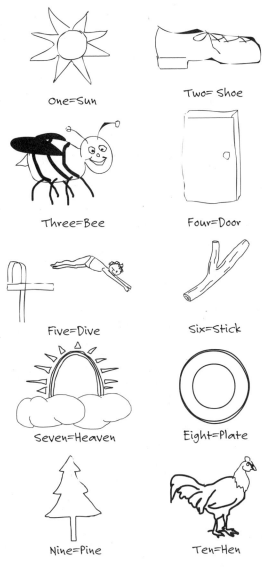

One=Sun

Two=Shoe

Three=Bee

Four=Door

Five=Dive

Six=Stick

Seven=Heaven

Eight=Plate

Nine=Pine

Ten=Hen

Figure 7.2
Visuals for a Number-Rhyme System

TYPES OF MEMORIZATION DEVICES

order, relate the item to be remembered to the rhyming picture associated with the number. For example, suppose in biology you need to remember the four steps of cellular respiration (glycolysis, transition reaction, Krebs cycle, and respiratory chain). You could hook each stage to the rhyming picture for that number, as illustrated in Figure 7.3.

- **Stage 1**: Glycolysis is the process of breaking down glucose, a sugar, to produce pyruvate. Therefore, the first rhyming image links the number one with "sun" and shows a sugary ice cream cone under a blazing sun.
- **Stage 2**: Transition reaction is the bridge between stages 1 and 3 in which pyruvate is converted to active acetate and CO_2 is released. Thus, the rhyming image links the number two with "two" and shows two tennis shoes, one old and beat-up, the other "transitioned" into a clean, new one.
- **Stage 3**: The Krebs cycle is where oxidative decarboxylation occurs. The rhyming image links the number three with "bees" and shows a bee hovering over a crib

Stage 1: Glycolysis represented by the sun melting a sugary ice cream cone.

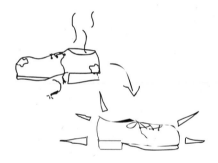

Stage 2: Transition reaction imaged with two shoes, one dirty with holes and the other changed or "transitioned" into a shiny, clean shoe with no holes.

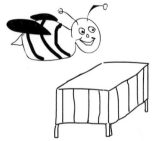

Stage 3: Krebs cycle triggered by the bee hovering over a crib.

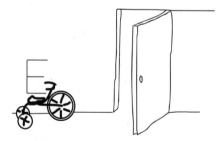

Stage 4: Electron transport system represented by a tricycle ridden by an E going through a door.

Figure 7.3
Number-Rhyme Images to Remember the Stages in Cellular Respiration

CHAPTER 7   USING MEMORIZATION TECHNIQUES

(*crib* sounds like *Krebs*).

- **Stage 4**: The respiratory chain or electron transport system involves electrons being passed from one carrier to another. The rhyming image links the number four with "door" and shows a tricycle ridden by an "E" (for electron transport) passing through the doorway.

Thus, to recall the four stages of cellular respiration, you need only to say and see the images shown in Figure 7.3.

Number-shape system A more visual processor might prefer to use the number-shape memory system to remember the stages of cellular respiration. A permanent memory foun-

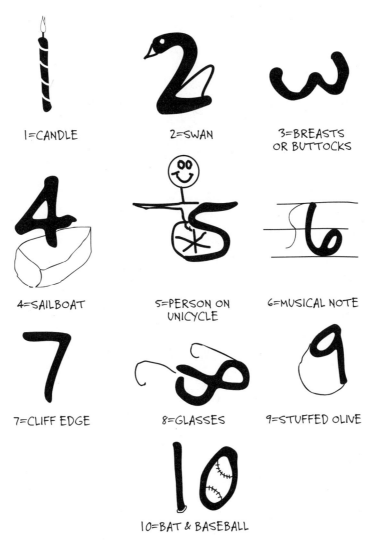

Figure 7.4
Number-Shape Memory System with the Visual Images

CREATING LOCI-BASED MEMORY SYSTEMS

Create your own loci-based memory system and use it to remember academic information for your classes as well as personal information.

dation like the one shown in Figure 7.4 works well for visual processors. To use this memory system, first create the permanent memory base in which the shape of the number suggests an actual physical object. Next, relate the picture associated with the number to the piece of information you want to remember. Figure 7.5 shows how you might apply the number-shape system to remember the four stages of cellular respiration. When you are ready to use the permanent memory base again, mentally wipe it clean of whatever you were last remembering and reuse the base.

Practicing the memory techniques that appeal to you will

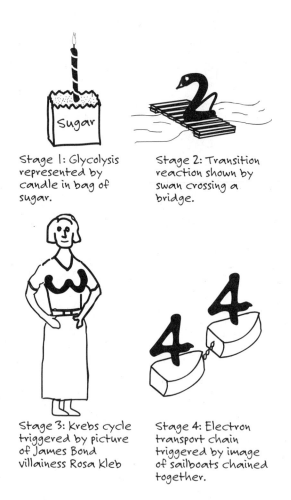

Stage 1: Glycolysis represented by candle in bag of sugar.

Stage 2: Transition reaction shown by swan crossing a bridge.

Stage 3: Krebs cycle triggered by picture of James Bond villainess Rosa Kleb.

Stage 4: Electron transport chain triggered by image of sailboats chained together.

Figure 7.5
Number-Shape Images to Remember the Stages in Cellular Respiration

increase your ability to remember things. Practice does not have to be just with school material. Try some of these techniques to help you remember people's phone numbers, to make a to-do list while you're driving to school, or to remember your student ID number.

Notes

[1]Sheila Ostrander and Lynn Schroeder, *Superlearning* (New York: Delacorte Press, 1980).

[2]Recited by a Beefeater guide at the Tower of London, England.

STUDYING FOR TESTS

Tips

1. Know what each test will cover, how many and what types of questions it will have, and how much it will count toward your final course grade.
2. List potential test topics in order from most to least important, and give the most study time to the important topics.
3. Spread your studying for a test over several days.
4. Use time management principles to plan your test preparation.
5. Organize study materials in different ways for better and quicker learning: FITS VOCAB notecards, diagrams, pictures, and basic organizational patterns.
6. Use mnemonic devices to help you remember key facts.
7. Prepare yourself physically by eating well, exercising, and getting enough sleep.
8. Do not try to learn a few more facts just before the exam.
9. Do a quick review right before the test.
10. Control minor test anxiety by doing deep breathing or visualizing a relaxing place.

A Left-Brained Overview

I. Developing Test Study Strategies
   A. Collect basic information about the test
   B. Set grade targets
   C. Predict possible test questions
   D. Prioritize study topics
   E. Focus on test question problem areas
II. Preparing a Study Plan
III. Organizing and Synthesizing Material to Be Studied
IV. Group Study and Group Tests
V. Cramming When You Must
   A. Survey test material
   B. Select only the main ideas and major supporting points
   C. Learn these WELL
VI. Final Test Preparations
   A. Productive cramming
   B. Mental and physical preparation
   C. Required or permitted test materials
VII. Coping with Test Anxiety
   A. Relaxation techniques
   B. Affirmations

A Right-Brained Overview

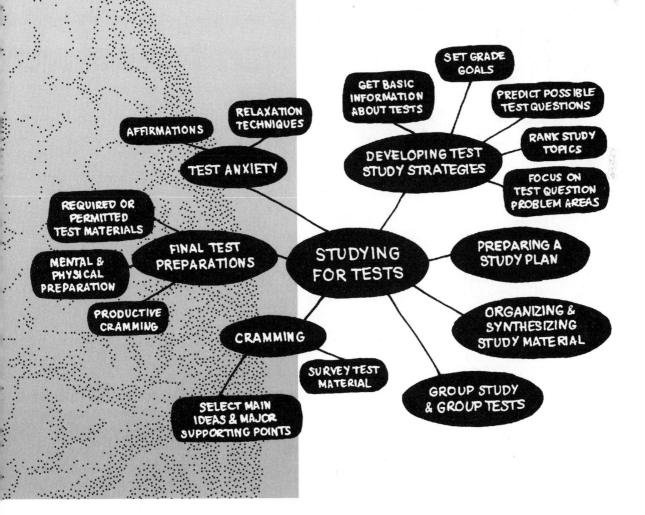

Midterms are coming and you discover that you have three exams the same week. Two require memorizing a lot of facts and details as well as understanding concepts. You're wondering how you can possibly be adequately prepared. In this chapter we will show you how to handle such multiple demands.

IS THIS YOU?

DEVELOPING TEST STUDY STRATEGIES

l. Getting Information About the Test

Your first step is to check through the syllabi and lecture notes of the classes you're being tested in. The more information you have about the tests, the better you will be able to plan effective study strategies. Look for answers to the following questions:

1. When is the test?
2. What chapters will it cover?
3. Will test questions be taken from both the text and the lectures?
4. Will test questions be taken equally from the text and the lectures? Or will one be emphasized more than the other? If so, which one?

5. What type of questions will be on the test (multiple-choice, true-false, matching, identification, short-answer, essay)?
6. How many questions will be on the test?
7. How much time will you have to answer the questions?
8. What is the value of the test in relation to your final course grade?
9. How will you be expected to answer the test questions (notepaper, blue book, computer sheet)?
10. What materials must you bring to the test? What optional items may you bring?

Figure 8.1 shows how you might gather information for a biology and a psychology exam.

	BIOLOGY	PSYCHOLOGY
Exam Date	Tues., Nov. 6	Fri., Nov. 9
Material Covered	7 Chapters 2, 3, 5, 6, 7, 9, 11	10 Chapters 1-10
Question Source	Text & Lecture	Text & Lecture
Question Type & No.	25 Multiple-choice 10 fill-ins 3 short answers	30 Multiple-choice 20 True-False 2 points each=100 pts.
Amount of Test Time	70 minute class =60 minutes of test time	50 minute class= 40 minutes test time
Test's Value	100 points 25% of final grade	$\frac{1}{3}$ of final course grade
How Answer Questions	On test itself	Computer answer sheet
Materials to Bring to Exam	1 page of BIO diagrams are OK	#2 pencil ? (nothing but brain)
No. of Study Hours Needed	4	5-6
Exam Grade Goal	High—A Lowest—B	High—A Lowest—A-

Figure 8.1
Sample Test Information-Gathering Chart

2. Setting Grade Targets

EXERCISE 8.1

GATHERING BASIC TEST INFORMATION

Collect information about one or more of your upcoming exams by answering the ten basic questions. Use Figure 8.1 as a model. You may want to combine this activity with Exercise 8.3.

When setting grade goals for individual tests, consider both your final grade goal for the course and any grades you've already earned. Think about whether you have the time and motivation to do the necessary work to reach your goal. For each test figure out the highest grade you believe you can earn in that course and how much studying you'll need to do to have a reasonable chance of achieving that grade. Then figure out the lowest grade you could earn on that test and still feel you have a chance of achieving your final grade goal for the entire course. By establishing a wider grade goal range, you have a better chance of being successful. Since success breeds more success, you are preparing for future success in your college courses.

3. Predicting Test Questions and Ranking Study Topics

Begin your exam study preparation by surveying all the material the test will cover. When surveying lecture notes, pay attention to topics that were emphasized during the lectures and to any items you coded as potential test questions (see Chapter 5 on note-taking for specific details). Figure 8.2 shows a portion of a left-brained survey chart for the psychology test. Figure 8.3 shows a right-brained way to do the same thing.

Now you can begin to prioritize the psychology topics into three study topic groups:

A Group—topics that were stressed in both the text and the lectures or that the instructor said would be on the test. It is almost certain that there will be quite a few questions from each of these topics on the test.

TEXTBOOK CHAPTERS	LECTURE NOTES

Research designs for studying dev.
 	
Dev. of thinking & reasoning
    Piaget's stages of dev. (5)
    Kohlberg's moral reasoning
Stages of language dev.
 	
Social & emotional dev.
Erikson's 8 stages of dev.
	Piaget's stages of dev.
	Perry's stages of moral dev.
	Erikson's stages of dev.
	Gilligan's stages of moral dev.
	Gender role dev.
	Adolescent sexuality
	Kübler-Ross's 5 stages of
	    adjustment to death

Figure 8.2
Sample Left-Brained Approach to Survey of Potential Psychology Test Material[1]

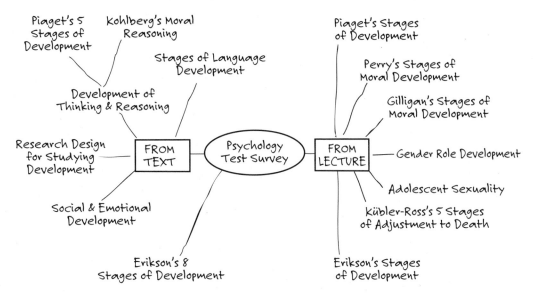

Figure 8.3
Sample Right-Brained Approach to Survey of Potential Psychology Test Material

B Group—topics that were stressed in either the text or the lectures. There is a high probability that the test will have some questions from each of these topics.

C Group—topics that were mentioned in either the text or the lectures but were not particularly stressed. A few questions will probably be taken from some of the topics in this group.

The priority study list for our sample psychology test looks like this:

A-Group Study Topics (*Expect a number of questions on both topics.*)
1. Theories about human stages of thinking and reasoning development
   a. Piaget's four stages of development
   b. Erikson's eight stages of development
2. Theories about moral stages of development
   a. Kohlberg's stages of moral reasoning development
   b. Perry's stages of moral development
   c. Gilligan's stages of moral development

Note: Piaget's and Erikson's theories were placed in the A group because the textbook devoted several pages to each topic and the instructor lectured in detail on each topic. Theories about moral development were included because the textbook stressed human development stages in general and the instructor lectured in detail on three theories of moral development. This means both author and instructor consider them important.

B-Group Study Topics (*Expect fewer questions on each of these topics than on A-group topics.*)
1. Social and emotional development
    a. Gender role development
    b. Adolescent sexuality
    c. Kübler-Ross's five stages of adjustment to death

Note: Topics were placed in the B group because they were emphasized in only one place, either the textbook or the lectures. They are important, but not as important as the A-group topics. If you study the topics in both the A and B groups, you will probably be able to answer 75–85 percent of the test questions easily.

C-Group Study Topics (*Expect a few questions about some of these topics.*)
1. Stages of human language development
2. Research designs for studying development

Note: These topics were placed on the C group instead of the B group because of the limited amount of time spent on them in lectures or the limited number of pages devoted to them in the text.

The preceding analysis of sample psychology test material was analyzed and prioritized in a traditional left-brained format. Figure 8.4 shows how the same prioritizing process might be done using a right-brained spidergram. Looking at the comparative spidergram, you can see major topics covered in both reading assignments and in the lectures. Topics covered in both are circled and linked by wavy lines while others are simply circled and linked. Topic groups also are ranked A, B, and C.

When you finish your psychology survey, you'll have a list of topics arranged in the order of importance for test study. Instead of beginning with the first chapter of the text or the first page of lecture notes, and working through sequentially, study first those topics you have categorized as A-group or top-priority topics. Then, focus on the B-group topics and finally on C-group topics.

4. Focusing on Test Question Problem Areas

At the same time you are surveying potential test material, also look for items that can "trick" or trip you up.

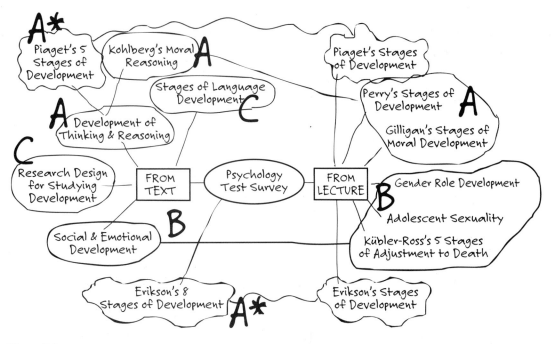

Figure 8.4
Sample Right-Brained Spidergram for Psychology Test Topic Prioritization

Similar or confusing terms or definitions Often terms that are very similar in spelling or pronunciation or meaning can be easily confused. When you encounter such terms while studying, take time to figure out a way to remember which is which. You won't have time to do it during the exam, and not being able to remember which is which may cause you problems on other test items. For example, consider the developmental psychology terms *accommodation* and *assimilation*. They can be confusing terms because both are long words, both begin with the letter *a*, and both deal with how people modify their behaviors or views of the word—their schema.

accommodation—Piaget's term for the way a person changes how s/he behaves or envisions the world (old schema) to include a new object or behavior (e.g., an infant will change how s/he sucks a bottle in order to suck a pacifier)

assimilation—Piaget's term for the way a person tries to apply already learned behaviors (old schema) to new objects (e.g., sucking on a new toy)[2]

If you haven't clearly differentiated between the two terms before the test, you might have some problems. To avoid this pitfall, spend a brief part of your study time making sure you

EXERCISE 8.2

SURVEYING POTENTIAL TEST MATERIAL

Survey the material you'll be tested on for one or more of your upcoming tests. Prioritize study topics into three groups, and identify any confusing terms and correct but illogical facts that might trip you up on the exam. Plan ways to clarify confusing terms or illogical facts.

can quickly and easily tell the difference between potentially confusing terms. You may find some of the memorization techniques described in Chapter 7 useful for this purpose.

Correct but illogical-sounding facts Every subject has true or correct facts that don't logically make sense. If you haven't taken a bit of time to clarify these for yourself before the test, they might throw you. Consider this bit of psychological information.

Eight- to 11-month-old infants seeing a toy hidden first on the left side and then on the right side will always reach for the right side.[3]

This is true, but if you haven't thought about it before the test, it might trip you up.

Note: The entire survey process should take between 45 minutes and an hour and a half.

PREPARING A STUDY PLAN

Once you've surveyed the test material, your next step is to plan how to integrate studying for the test into your regular weekly schedule. A sample study plan is shown in Figure 8.5. Note that when studying for a test, you need to integrate principles of effective time management, learning, and test preparation. Specifically, do the following:

EXERCISE 8.3

PLANNING FOR TEST STUDY TIME

After collecting information about one or more of your upcoming tests, plan study time and put it in your regular schedule. You may wish to do this in conjunction with Exercise 8.1.

1. Distribute test study time for better retention rather than cramming preparation into one or two long study periods.
2. Continue with your regular class schedule and study plans instead of cutting classes and not doing regular reading and homework. This way you won't get behind in other classes.
3. Maintain your regular exercise program and eat at least two nutritious meals a day to keep physically prepared.

	Monday	Tuesday	Wednesday	Thursday	Friday	Saturday	Sunday
8:00	Study Bio test (1 hr.)	Work on English essay	Study Student Success test	Type English essay	Work on Math	WORK	Breakfast with kids
9:00	English Class	MATH	English Class	MATH	English Class		& friends
10:00	Psych	Final Review Bio test	Psych	Proofread English essay	Psych		Church
11:00	Student Success	BIO	Student Success	BIO	Student Success	8—4	F U N
12:00	Lunch		Lunch		Lunch		T I M E
	Prep for Bio lab	Lunch	1. Study Psych test (30 min)	Lunch	1. Review week's class Notes		
1:00	BIO Lab	1—5 WORK	2. Work on Math (1 hr)	1—5 WORK	2. Plan next week's schedule		
2:00			Drive to kids' school / Joshua's Parent-Teacher Conference		Personal free time— Reward		
3:00	Brainstorm topics & ideas for English essay / Study BIO	Break / Darcy's Parent-Teacher Conference			for sticking with time schedule		Survey & Prep for Psych test
4:00	test (1½ hrs.)		Go to Park with Kids		all week (Kids are visiting Mom on	Pick up kids; go home	Prep for College Success class
5:00	Pick up kids Do dinner Evening stuff 1. Study BIO	Same schedule M–Thurs.			Fridays after school & Saturdays	F	Study for BIO test
P.M.	2. Read Student Success 3. Work on Math	1. Study Psych test 1½ hrs. 2. Work Eng. Essay	1. Study Psych test 1½ hrs. 2. Work Eng. Essay	1. Study Psych test (1½ hrs.) Do final Review 2. Work Eng. Essay		U N	

Figure 8.5
Sample Weekly Schedule Incorporating Test Study Time

ORGANIZING AND SYNTHESIZING MATERIAL TO BE STUDIED

There is no one correct way to organize and synthesize test material. You need to learn a number of ways to organize, synthesize, and relate information so that you can use the technique that is most appropriate to a specific subject or most workable for you. For example, in preparing for a psychology test, you might do the following:

1. Create FITS VOCAB cards for all the psychology terms to be precisely defined (see the FITS VOCAB formula in Chapter 6).

2. Write potential study questions as part of the process of revising lecture notes (see Chapter 5).
3. Use subject organizational patterns to relate subject material (see Chapter 4). A sample comparison and contrast chart of Piaget's and Erikson's stages of development is shown in Figure 8.6.

Note that Figure 8.6 not only summarizes the information but also compares the two theories of human development. The chart makes it possible to see similarities and differences between the two theories. To support this form of learning, you might also create FITS VOCAB cards for each development stage named by Piaget and Erikson. These cards will give you

Erikson	Piaget
0-3: Trust vs mistrust (learning to trust primary caregivers)	0-1½: Sensorimotor stage (motor responses)
1-3: Autonomy vs shame & doubt (concerned with doing things independently)	1½-7: Preoperational stage (language learning & oneway irreversible concepts)
3-6: Initiative vs guilt (concerned with morality & acceptability of own actions)	7-11: Concrete Operations Stage (more of a literal thinking stage)
6-12: Industry vs Inferiority (concerned with own value)	
Early teens: Identity vs role confusion (concerned w/discovering independent identity)	11 on: Formal Operations Stage (abstract, hypothetical thinking)
Late teens: Intimacy vs isolation (concerned with type of adult lifestyle to have)	
Late 20s-retirement: Generativity vs stagnation (concerned with value of individual's life)	
After retirement: Ego integrity vs despair (concerned with reflecting on value of one's life)	

Figure 8.6
Sample Comparison and Contrast Chart for Organizing and Synthesizing Psychology Test Material

ORGANIZING AND SYNTHESIZING TEST MATERIAL

Organize, synthesize, and relate some or all of the information you've collected for one or more of your upcoming exams. If you choose to, make some mnemonics for the most important chunks of information.

in-depth information to integrate with the broader overview contained in the comparison and contrast chart. The time it takes to make such a chart is valuable study time because you have to select relevant information about the two theories from the text and lecture notes and hold this information in your short-term memory—which is how knowledge is transferred from short- to long-term memory. The writing of the chart is a kinesthetic activity, and the chart itself is visual, making it a powerful learning tool for both kinesthetic and visual learners. If you are an auditory learner, you can recite the information aloud as well.

Other ways to organize subject information for test study are discussed in detail in the following chapters:

FITS VOCAB cards—Chapter 6

Spidergrams—Chapter 6

Idea clustering—Chapter 6

Mnemonics (memory cues)—Chapter 7

Organizational patterns—Chapter 4

GROUP STUDY AND GROUP EXAMS

Some students like to study with other students. This can be an effective way to prepare for tests, but you need to study by yourself first and then check and reinforce your understanding while working with the study group. Students who study together regularly find it useful to have different group members prepare one topic to teach to the others. Another effective group technique is for each group member to write several test questions. Then, the group can practice answering test questions.

If you are taking a group exam, your group needs to plan beforehand how you will take the exam. Will each group member read the test questions and answer as many as possible and then consult with other group members? Or will the group read and answer each question together? How will you resolve a conflict if group members don't agree on an answer? How will your group handle the not uncommon situation in which one group member is coasting and relying on the hard work and knowledge of other group members to get through the course? As more and more instructors incorporate cooperative learning techniques into the classroom, you will need to develop interpersonal skills to learn to work effectively with others.

EXERCISE 8.5

PRACTICING CRAMMING

Use the cramming technique just described to collect basic information about one of your upcoming tests so you'll know how it's done. Then, since you'll certainly be doing this long before your test, go ahead and study in depth. Or, practice the cramming technique by helping a friend who's procrastinated and has a test tomorrow.

CRAMMING

Like all educators we don't recommend cramming as your normal study pattern. However, we know that at least occasionally in your college career you'll misjudge your time needs or get blindsided by an unexpected test or simply fall behind. In such situations you'll have to cram. But there is a right way and a wrong way to cram. Simply put, if the test is tomorrow and you have not read one page of the eighteen chapters of the subject you'll be tested on, you're not going to pull off an A and you can't learn everything. Instead, survey the material you're being tested on, select the main ideas and the major supporting points, and *learn these*. Also, for each chapter choose ten vocabulary terms that closely relate to the main ideas and major supporting points. Spend what time you have learning these ideas, supporting points, and vocabulary terms as well as you can. It will probably be enough to get you a passing grade. Then, don't let yourself get in this situation again. Cramming can bail you out of a tight spot, but it's no substitute for real learning, and you're not spending huge amounts of money or putting in lots of time for this type of result.

FINAL TEST PREPARATIONS

The final study session before an exam is a productive cramming study session devoted to reviewing information already studied, not trying to learn any new material. Your goal in this session is to clarify or more firmly fix in your memory the already reviewed information.

Since test-taking is both a physical and mental performance, you need to prepare yourself physically as well as mentally. Good physical preparation includes adequate sleep and nutritious food as well as a continuation of your normal physical exercise regimen. It is especially important during finals when many students are prone to pull all-nighters or skip meals to maintain a schedule that includes some regular sleep and two regular meals daily. Without sleep and adequate food (not pop, chips, and donuts), your body and mind will switch to slow mode and you'll be inefficient at both learning and remembering what you've studied. A general rule of thumb is that if it comes out of a vending machine or a fast food place, it may not be the best food for learning and remembering.

Your last meal before an exam should be high in protein and low in sugar and simple carbohydrates. Protein metabolizes slowly over an extended time period and provides the type of fuel that promotes concentration and thinking. Too much sugar or simple carbohydrates will calm and relax you to the point that you may not function at an optimal level during the test—or even care whether you do or not.

The day of the test, plan so that you get ready without rushing and arrive a few minutes early at the classroom. You do not want to increase your anxiety due to lateness. Note, too, that mild exercise prior to a test can increase physical alertness and result in a better performance. Try walking briskly to your test. Also, be sure to bring all required as well as any permitted materials to class. We recommend that you bring extra pens or pencils as well. And even if you do not anticipate needing them, if they are allowed bring dictionaries, notes, or other such items with you. They act as a security blanket. As permitted, you might also bring gum or mints. If you are slightly ill, bring tissues, nasal spray, and the like. If you are more than slightly ill and you have established yourself as a good student, discuss the situation with your instructor. He or she might allow you to wait until you recovered to take the test.

When you arrive in the test room, select a seat that is as free from distractions as possible. This means avoiding glaring or flickering lights and drafts of cold or hot air as well as classmates who have such annoying habits as chewing gum, talking to themselves during a test, or clicking their pens. It also means removing yourself from friends with whom you might be tempted to exchange words or looks. (The instructor might interpret such behavior as cheating. Therefore, avoid any and all suspicious behavior.)

COPING WITH TEST ANXIETY

While waiting for the exam to begin, do not discuss or listen to other students discuss what was or was not studied. There is absolutely nothing you can do at this point to change what you did or did not study. It is better, therefore, not to drive up your anxiety level by telling yourself that you are doomed to failure before the test begins. Your attitude going into a test is vitally important to how well you do. If you think you are going to fail or do poorly, then you can make that happen. Maintain a positive attitude! Spend a few minutes reviewing in your mind material you have already thoroughly studied. Do NOT try to learn a few more bits of new information, skim over the textbook, or reread lecture notes. You will only confuse yourself. Also, try a relaxation technique to reduce test anxiety.

Here are some simple calming techniques you can do in public without raising eyebrows or causing people to look at you suspiciously. To get the fullest effect from these techniques, you need to practice them regularly.

- **Relaxing breathing**. Sit quietly and comfortably. Take a deep breath, all the way to the bottom of your diaphragm. Hold it for a second or two. Then, slowly release it and at the same time imagine that some of your tension is escaping with the breath. Do this several times to calm yourself.

- **Relaxing visualizing**. Sit quietly and comfortably. Close your eyes and begin to visualize a favorite place where you feel very comfortable and relaxed. Imagine the sights and sounds and smells of the place. Picture yourself walking about; notice how it feels to imagine yourself there. For a few minutes, focus on how relaxed you feel. Then, return to the classroom, bringing with you that feeling of relaxation.

- **Affirmations**. Either in tandem with one of the above exercises or on its own, try saying affirmations to yourself. An affirmation is simply a positive statement about yourself. In this case, we recommend that you give yourself an affirmation related to the upcoming test. You might tell yourself how prepared you are or how you are going to remain calm. Or you might remind yourself of one of the general principles of test-taking that you want to follow. Some sample affirmations are:

  I will follow my plan when taking the test.

  I will read and answer all questions I know, leaving the ones I don't know or am uncertain about blank.

  I have prepared carefully, and I will do my best.

  I will read the directions before beginning to answer questions.

  I will read true-false questions carefully, looking for absolutes and spoilers (see Chapter 9).

  Affirmations give you a focal point as well as a way to program positive thinking and positive action.

Note: If you are interested in some other easy-to-use and workable relaxation techniques, look at Herbert Benson's

Relaxation Response (New York: Avon Books, 1976) or check with your local book or music store or school library for guided relaxation and visualization tapes (a popular visualization tape is *Creative Visualization* by Shakta Gawain).

If you experience more than simple nervousness before a test, then you may need to take further action. There are a number of audiotapes designed to help people control test anxiety. Your school's counseling center may offer a workshop or group on the topic. Another option is to see a counselor or psychologist for individual work on the problem. Finally, it may help you to know that test anxiety or exam phobia is a common problem for a number of people. However, if you always freeze up before a test and get lower grades than your knowledge and studying would indicate, then consult with a professional to assess the problem and plan ways to deal with it.

Notes

[1] Information on stages of human development adapted from James W. Kalat, *Introduction to Psychology*, 2nd ed. (Belmont, CA: Wadsworth, 1990).

[2] Kalat, p. 194.

[3] Kalat, p. 196.

TAKING OBJECTIVE TESTS

Tips

A Left-Brained Overview

A Right-Brained Overview

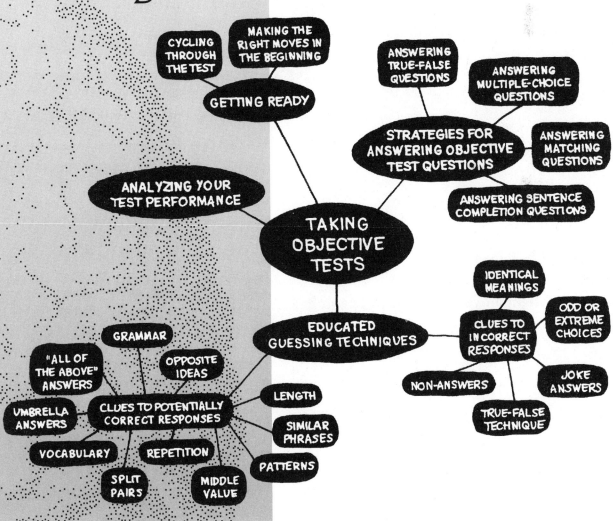

You've studied hard and you think you know the material. However, you're a little concerned about the format of the test. You suspect that there might be types of questions that you're not familiar with, and you're worried about how to budget your time so that you complete the test. In this chapter we'll show you how to take all types of objective tests—and how to take an educated guess when you're not sure about an answer.

IS THIS YOU?

GETTING READY

Making the Right Moves at the Test's Beginning

As soon as you receive your copy of the test, scan it for the following information:

- Total number of questions
- Different types of questions and the value of each type
- Any special instructions (for example, "Answer 10 of the 15" or "Mark true and false answers with + for true and 0 for false")

Most importantly, read all the test directions, make sure you understand them, and follow them exactly. Use the following test-taking guidelines.

1. **Allot test time for each question type in relation to the total value of the questions**. Suppose you have a ninety-question, 50-minute psychology test. Subtracting 10 minutes of test time for your instructor to get things started, you have 40 minutes to work on the test. Your estimations of how much time to allot to each section would be based on the total point value for that set of test questions:

50 multiple-choice
    questions $\times$ 1 pt. each = 50 possible pts. = 19 minutes
20 true-false
    questions $\times \frac{1}{2}$ pt. each = 10 possible pts. = 5 minutes
20 matching
    questions $\times$ 2 pts. each = 40 possible pts. = 12 minutes

      TOTAL TEST
    POINTS POSSIBLE = 100   TOTAL TIME = 36 minutes

Based on your calculations, you've accounted for 36 minutes of test time. The remaining 4 minutes are reserved for filling in any unanswered questions and for finishing up the test. Remember, you don't need to do extensive math calculations here, but rather some quick estimations so that you have a reasonable idea of how to spend your precious test time.

2. **Answer question types in the order you are most comfortable with**. For instance, you might like to start with *true-false* questions because they go fairly quickly, or you might prefer to save them for last for the same reason. Similarly, you might choose to start with *multiple-choice* questions because they take longer and often are worth a lot of points, or you might prefer to do another question type first in order to warm up for the multiple-choice. Since well-written *matching* questions contain lots of factual information, you may be able to use them to jog your memory of other types. Thus, it's a good idea to skim them quickly before you begin answering the other types. However, don't answer them until you've warmed up because if you make one mistake in matching you'll no doubt make at least two. Finally, for the same reasons, you'll probably want to skim the *sentence completion* items to see what's being asked but delay answering them until you're warmed up.

There's no one correct order in which to answer questions. Become aware of what you are most comfortable with and use that pattern. For our sample psychology test, you might follow this plan:

1. Skim the matching questions.
2. Begin answering the multiple-choice questions because they are worth half the possible test points and you feel you can handle them better at the test's beginning.

139

3. Move to the matching questions because they are worth 40 points.
4. End with the true-false questions because they aren't worth many points, and in a time pinch you can get through them quickly.

Cycling Through the Test

Other than reading and following test directions, the most important principle of effective test-taking is to cycle through the test, answering questions in the following manner: The first time you read through the test questions, read as fast as you comfortably can and answer in one of three ways:

1. If you know the answer, then mark your answer sheet.
2. If you are semi-sure of the answer but are not sure enough to choose a final answer, then mark the question in some way to show this. If the instructor has asked you not to mark on the test, ask permission to use scratch paper. Number it and mark known and semi-known answers.
3. If you don't know or remember the answer, mark nothing. Do not waste valuable test time reading and rereading the question; rather, move on to the next question. On the first read-through, don't panic when you leave a lot of questions unanswered. You need to warm up to the task of test-taking.

On your second pass through the test questions, attempt to answer only those you marked as partially known on the first read-through. Do not even read the unknown questions. This will save valuable test time, and you'll remember more answers the second time through because you're now warmed up.

On the third and all subsequent read-throughs, try to answer any unanswered questions. Sometime after the third or fourth read-through, consider that for whatever reason you will not be able to answer some of these questions. Therefore, begin to apply the educated guessing principles explained later in this chapter.

About 2–5 minutes before the test ends, stop trying to answer any remaining unanswered questions. If you haven't figured out the answer by now, then you aren't going to. It's time to go into the final step. Cover the test questions with your answer sheet; review your answers to make sure that you have marked only one answer and that you've erased all stray marks. Deal with any unanswered questions depending on how the test will be scored.

1. If the test will be graded using a penalty for guessing or a correction-for-chance formula (one whereby a percent-

age of the number of questions answered incorrectly is subtracted from the number of questions answered correctly; items left blank are not included in this formula), then either be very cautious when guessing or do not guess. It may be to your advantage to leave these last few questions blank.

2. If there is no penalty for guessing, then GUESS. Fill in every blank. If you know nothing about the instructor's test-writing patterns (discussed in the section "Analyzing Your Test Performance" later in the chapter), follow this pattern of automatic responses:

C, C, B for multiple-choice; repeat as necessary.

T, T, F for true-false; repeat as necessary.

These automatic responses are not guaranteed to work every time, nor are they necessarily the best choices. We recommend the *C-C-B* pattern simply because more correct answers are placed in those positions in multiple-choice items. Similarly, true-false questions tend to have more true than false answers. Choose your own individual automatic response to use in the final moments of a test. The important thing is to have a plan for the final, precious, all-too-few moments of the test.

STRATEGIES FOR ANSWERING OBJECTIVE TEST QUESTIONS

Objective tests might contain multiple-choice, true-false, matching, and fill-in or sentence-completion questions. They are "objective" because, unlike an essay or subjective test, such questions have a single predetermined correct answer. In dealing with objective-test questions, follow these general guidelines:

1. **Use logic**. Applying logic is always a powerful test-taking tool. Consider this biology question:

   Populations grow exponentially when _____
   a. birth rate remains above death rate and neither changes
   b. death rate remains above birth rate
   c. immigration and emigration rates are equal (a zero value)
   d. emigration rates exceed immigration rates
   e. both *a* and *c* combined are correct

   In thinking about growing populations, you realize that answers *b* and *d* would result in decreasing populations.

Tossing those two out leaves you with *a, c,* and *e.* Logically, *a* would result in an increase but *c* could be a contributory factor. Therefore, *e* is the best choice. (Yes, it's correct.)[1]

2. **Draw on other knowledge**. Apply any facts you know or information you have to improve your chances of choosing the correct answer.

3. **Define or restate questions in your own words.** Rephrasing the question in your own words, defining terms, and stating what the question is seeking, all clarify the question and sometimes suggest the correct answer. It also sometimes helps to substitute synonyms in both the stem and the potential answers.

4. **Visualize**. When appropriate, draw a picture of the problem, either mentally or literally. This is very useful in science and math and especially appropriate for visual learners. Often, it's possible to deduce logically the answer from the diagram.

Answering True-False Questions

True-false questions are easy for many test-takers but tricky for others. Although there are only two possible answers, true-false questions test both your subject knowledge and your ability to read and comprehend the language. Many times what makes a true-false question correct or incorrect depends on how it is phrased. Therefore, you must read such questions carefully, being on the lookout especially for qualifying words and spoilers.

Qualifying words tell how much or how often something is involved. Typical qualifiers are *some, most, generally,* and *usually.* **Absolutes** are qualifying words or ways of phrasing that mean that the subject under discussion either *always* or *never* has a certain characteristic. Typical absolutes include the following:

absolute	inordinately
absolutely	irrefutable
all	inviolable
always	never
axiomatic	only
categorical	peculiarly
completely	positive
doubtless	quite
entirely	self-evident
forever	sole
immeasurable	totally
inalienable	unchallenged

incontestable	unchangeable
incontrovertible	undeniable
indefinitely	undoubtedly
indisputable	unequivocal
indubitably	unexceptional
inevitable	unimpeachable
inexorable	unqualified
infallible	unquestionably
infinite	wholly
inflexible	without exception

In nonscience subjects, a true-false question with either a stated or an implied absolute is false 99 percent of the time. Consider these true-false items, each of which contains a stated absolute and each of which is false:

1. There is *only* one method for solving a science problem.
2. Ethics means doing that which is legally correct *without exception.*
3. In any number of coin tosses, heads will *always* come up the same number of times as tails.
4. *All* students who graduate in the top 25 percent of their high school classes go to college and earn high grades.

More difficult to spot than stated absolutes are *implied* absolutes, wherein items are worded in such a way that they imply that everything in the named group always or never has that characteristic. What if the four true-false statements are written without the absolute words?

1. There is one method for solving a science problem.
2. Ethics means doing that which is legally correct.
3. In any number of coin tosses, heads will come up the same number of times as tails.
4. Students who graduate in the top 25 percent of their high school classes go to college and earn high grades.

Notice that even without the absolute word, all four items are false because, as written, each statement means that everyone or everything in the group is always the same. Here are the same statements with less than 100 percent qualifying terms:

1. There is one method used *most often* for solving a science problem.
2. Ethics *generally* means doing that which is legally correct.

FINDING ABSOLUTES AND SPOILERS

Read through old true-false test questions to spot stated and implied absolutes and spoilers. Check the correct answers. Such practice will increase your ability to spot absolutes and spoilers when actually taking a test.

3. In any number of coin tosses, heads will *usually* come up the same number of times as tails.
4. *Many* students who graduate in the top 25 percent of their high school classes go to college and earn high grades.

With only slight rephrasing, each of the four statements is now true.

The second language element to be alert to in true-false questions is the **spoiler**—the one incorrect fact that makes an otherwise correct statement false. In order for a true-false item to be true, all parts of the statement, no matter how trivial seeming, must be true. In essence, a true-false question is itself an absolute. Therefore, one incorrect name, one wrong date, or even one misspelled word could make a true-false item false.

Spoilers have a nasty habit of hiding in a large amount of information or appearing near the end of the statement. Often, test-takers are in such a hurry to get through the test that they read true-false statements too quickly. The eyes see the words, but the brain doesn't process the meaning. To counteract this, read true-false statements carefully for meaning and be on the lookout for spoilers. During the test don't read at a snail's pace, but do read slowly enough to ensure comprehension.

The following true-false item presents problems because it is long and packed with details.

If Romanesque architecture tended to be monastery-based, that of the Gothic was more allied to the growing cities, and the Gothic church featured higher naves, larger stained-glass windows, and the use of flying buttresses and rounded arches.

An efficient way to handle such a question is to break it into small information chunks and check the accuracy of the facts in each chunk. For example, take the first part of the item ("If Romanesque architecture tended to be monastery based . . ."). Is that part true or false? Then, check the next chunk ("Gothic was more allied to the growing cities"). True or false? If each chunk is true, then the entire item must be true. But if even one small chunk is false, then the entire item must be false.

Answering Multiple-Choice Questions

One major challenge in taking multiple-choice tests is the amount of reading involved with each question. Not only is this time-consuming, but reading and rereading the same question can be confusing. When you read a multiple-choice item, ask yourself the following:

1. What is the basic *subject*?
2. What *time periods* or *dates* are given?
3. What *locations* are given?
4. Can you concentrate on any one *person* or *group* of people?
5. Are you given specific *directions* or a specific *focus*?

To illustrate how this process works, let's analyze a sample multiple-choice item from a history class.

The major single reason for the dramatic reduction of immigration to the USA in the 1920s was _____

a. Johnson-Reed Act
b. Great Depression
c. unemployment in the USA
d. improved economic conditions in Germany and Poland

Once you've read the question analytically, then read the responses. If you are absolutely certain of the correct answer, then mark it and go on to the next question. However, this usually will not be the case. Thus, concentrate first on eliminating responses that you are sure are incorrect.

You might eliminate responses using the following reasoning:

a. Johnson-Reed Act. You're not really sure about this, so you leave it as an option for the moment.

b. Great Depression. You know that the Great Depression began with the stock market crash of 1929 and continued through the 1930s. Since the question asks about the 1920s before the Great Depression occurred, *b* cannot be the answer. Eliminate this choice.

c. unemployment in the USA. You know further that there was a lot of unemployment during the Depression, but not in the 1920s. That was a boom time, the Roaring Twenties. It's not an accurate description of what was happening to employment in the 1920s. Eliminate this choice, too.

d. improved economic conditions in Germany and Poland. If economic conditions were improved, then reduced immigration could have resulted. But, in the 1920s economic conditions weren't much better in either Germany or Poland, so this doesn't seem to be the correct answer.

In this case the correct answer appears to be *a*. In actuality, the Johnson-Reed Act was the legislation that implemented ethnic and nationality quotas in the American immigration system.

This may seem like a lot of time-consuming steps, but you will do most of the steps together. Some of the time you will automatically and subconsciously notice these facts. In longer, more complicated questions, you may need consciously to pick out these points. In any event, in the long run reading multiple-choice questions analytically will help you find the correct answer more quickly.

Answering Matching Questions

Matching questions present challenges because of the amount of reading required, the greater number of potential answers to be considered, and the guarantee that if you make one mistake, you'll make at least a second one. Therefore, you're generally better off tackling matching questions after warming up on other question types first. However, always skim matching questions when you preview the test because well-written matching questions are a gold mine of information for jogging your memory or actually answering other test questions.

To begin answering matching questions, determine the following rules of the matching game:

1. How many questions and how many answers are there? It is helpful to know if there are an equal number of questions and answers or if some extra answers are included.
2. How many times may each answer be used? Some matching tests permit only a single use of each answer while others allow each answer to be used more than once.
3. How many answers are necessary per question to be considered a correct answer? Usually one answer is enough, but in some matching tests you must give more than one answer for each question to get the question correct.
4. Are there matching subsets within the larger matching test? Since matching tests usually contain the definitions of terms pertaining to major subject concepts, there often are two or more closely related matching questions. Some test-takers find it easier to sort out and answer three related questions rather than fifteen or more questions on different topics.
5. How are the matching answers to be recorded? Check the instructions on this point. Some tests specify capital letters only. Follow the directions exactly.

EXERCISE 9.4

PRACTICING ANSWERING MATCHING QUESTIONS

Try your hand at answering matching questions by matching the items shown below. The answers appear at the end of the chapter.

In actually answering matching questions, you can do several things. First, to save test time and to aid in recalling answers, use the column that contains the longer statements as your test questions and search the shorter column for answers. Second, to avoid wasting valuable test time reading material, mark off items as you answer them. Finally, if you end up with two unanswered questions and two answers and can't figure out which goes with which, put the same answer in both questions. You'll have a reasonable chance of getting one correct.

Matching Test

1. Social Psychologist
2. Biological Psychologist
3. Behavioral Psychologist
4. Cognitive Psychologist
5. Quantitative Psychologist
6. Psychoanalytic Psychologist
7. Humanistic Psychologist

a. Believes people make deliberate, conscious decisions about behaviors; cannot reduce humans to simple behaviors

b. Explains behavior in terms of activity of brain and other body organs

c. Measures individual differences and applies statistical procedures to determine meaning of measurements

d. Studies observable behaviors; concentrates on how behavior is learned

e. Studies how others influence an individual's actions, attitudes, emotions, and thought processes

f. Studies thought processes and knowledge acquisition

g. Treats psychological disorders by focusing on conscious and unconscious thoughts[2]

Answering Sentence Completion Questions

Sentence completion or fill-in-the-blank questions are a mix of the objective and subjective. They are objective in that they usually have one correct response, but subjective in that you have to recall the information without the benefit of looking at several responses. Before answering fill-in questions, determine the following:

1. Will you receive credit for only the exact term or for an explanation? If you are receiving credit only for the exact term, do not waste valuable test time writing out explanations of what you mean.

EXERCISE 9.5

PRACTICING SENTENCE COMPLETION ITEMS

Read some sentence completion questions from tests you've taken and identify any who? what? when? and where? facts and any how? or why? information.

2. Is the score for the sentence completion section calculated by the number of questions or the number of blanks? This may make a difference in terms of the total point value of the section and thus the development of your test-taking strategy.

3. Does only one term go in each blank? Some matching tests have more than one correct answer per blank. Sometimes you must get all answers to be marked correct.

4. Are the answer blanks all the same size? Blanks are sometimes a clue to the length of the correct answer. However, this is something that most test-writers easily correct by making sure all blanks are the same length.

5. Do the articles *a/an* appear before answer blanks? If the test-writer does not correct this by using *a(n)* before the blank, it can be a clue to whether the correct answer begins with a vowel or a consonant. However, this is being used less and less in tests.

When answering sentence completion questions, read the statement carefully, noting factual answers to who? what? when? and where? questions. Check as well to see if the statement answers how? and why? questions, because these can be powerful memory joggers. Consider the following sentence completion test item:

_____ was a late-nineteenth–early-twentieth-century Viennese psychoanalyst who developed the theory that the personality was composed of the ego, the id, and the superego; developed the technique of free association; and theorized that human psychological development moves through five stages—oral, anal, phallic, latency, and genital.

As you read the item, mentally mark the following information:

WHEN
_____ was a <u>late-nineteenth–early-twentieth-century</u>

WHERE **WHAT** **REMAINDER OF QUESTION**
<u>Viennese psychoanalyst</u> who <u>developed the theory that the</u>

PROVIDES INFORMATION ON WHY THIS PERSON WAS
<u>personality was composed of the ego, the id, and the super-</u>

NOTEWORTHY
<u>ego; developed the techniques free association; and theorized</u>
<u>that psychological development moves through five stages—</u>
<u>oral, anal, phallic, latency, and genital.</u>

WRITING YOUR OWN OBJECTIVE TEST QUESTIONS

Another way to sharpen your test-taking skills is to practice writing objective test questions. Either individually or in a group, write one or two multiple-choice, true-false, matching, and sentence completion test questions. Practice answering the questions. Ask your instructor if he or she is willing to use student-written questions on your tests. If so, write one question per 3 × 5 notecard. Include the correct answer and the source. This is also a great way to study in a group.

Paying attention to the when? where? and what? helps you weed out whole groups of psychologists because they lived at different times or places. The second half of the question helps you focus on the one psychoanalyst among several who lived at that time and worked in Vienna and who developed those psychological theories—Sigmund Freud.

ANALYZING YOUR TEST PERFORMANCE

When tests are given back, many students look at the grade and then put the test away, never to be examined again. Typically, the lower the grade, the less they analyze their test performance. However, test performance analysis is exactly the prescription for improving your future test performances. To analyze your test performance, answer these questions.

1. **How many questions of each type were missed?** Do you tend to miss more questions of one type (for example, true-false as opposed to multiple-choice)? If so, then focus on improving your performance on that type of exam question. This is more productive than simply trying to do better in general.

2. **What is the instructor's answer pattern?** Test-writers are human, and most tend to have a test-writing style. Count how many of the true-false questions were answered correctly with true and how many false. The general test-writing tendency is to write more statements that can be correctly answered true, but some instructors lean toward more false. Also count how many multiple-choice items were correctly answered a, b, c, d, and e. The general tendency is to put more correct answers in the middle positions (b and c). Once you know a particular instructor's answer pattern, you can adjust your automatic response pattern accordingly. For example, if your instructor seems to write more items correctly answered as false, then, when filling in unanswered test questions at the end of

the test, put *false* in every blank. If your instructor prefers *b* as a correct multiple-choice answer, then consider putting *b* in all remaining blanks just before you turn in your test.

3. **Why did you miss each question that you got wrong on the test?** This may seem obvious—you didn't know the answer. But it's not that simple. Reread each missed question and figure out why you missed it. You are looking for a pattern. Typical reasons for missing test questions include the following:

- **You didn't know the answer.** Does this happen frequently? Perhaps you simply need to study harder.
- **You studied the material but forgot it.** What didn't work about how you studied for this test? What changes can you make to improve your test preparation and performance on the next test?
- **You didn't study that information because it didn't seem important or there wasn't enough time.** What signals are you missing about what's important in the lectures and textbook? How can you change your time management plans so that you'll have enough test study time?
- **You misunderstood the question.** Is this your fault or was this an unclearly written question? If it happened only once or twice, it's probably not worth worrying about. But if it happens more frequently, you need to take a close look at why you are not "seeing eye to eye" with the test writer.
- **You misread the question.** Are you in too big a hurry to get through the test? Do you misread only certain types of questions, for example, true-false? Does this happen often? If so, practice answering the type of question that gives you trouble.
- **You didn't read the entire question.** Do you tend to mark the *first* correct answer you come to? For questions where the correct answer is "All of the above" or "Both *a* and *c*," this habit can cost you many test points.
- **You didn't see the "except" or "not" in the question.** How many questions of this type did you miss? If it's more than one or two, then devise a statement to remind yourself to pay particular attention to the "not" and "except" in questions.
- **You marked the right answer in the wrong answer place.** How come? Were you in too big a hurry? Did it happen only once or is this a typical behavior? If it's the latter, then think about why you let this happen and how you can change the behavior. Next time, just before taking a test, say to yourself, "I will mark my answers in the right spot."

- **The question was ambiguous**. During the test did you need to ask for clarification from the instructor? Do not decide on your own what she or he meant. Ask.

Once such test behaviors are discovered, you can easily change them and make a major difference in your test scores. Note, however, that it is more productive to work on changing one or two test behaviors at a time rather than trying to go from being an average or poor test-taker to being a spectacular one. You have a better chance of becoming a superior test-taker by improving one or two behaviors at a time.

4. **Where did most of the test questions come from?** Skim through your textbook. Does your instructor tend to write test questions based on the information in main headings and subheadings? What about any material highlighted by **boldface**, *italics*, or underlining? or information presented in lists, charts, diagrams, tables, captions, chapter summaries, or end-of-chapter questions? In lectures check whether you missed nonverbal signals from your instructor, such as writing information on the board, using an overhead, repeating information, or making eye contact with the class. Often, an alert note-taker can tune in to an instructor's nonverbals and become very aware of what lecture information that instructor considers important. Usually, what the lecturer considers important has a good chance of showing up as a test question. Learning where a particular instructor tends to take test questions from will enable you to study the right material for the test. (See Chapter 5, "Taking Lecture Notes," for detailed information on instructor nonverbals.)

5. **What were your three main problems on this test?** After analyzing the test, decide what gave you the most trouble or where your test-taking mistakes were. Yes, you may have more than three, but if you isolate the three major problems and work to correct them, then you can focus on three more the next time. Continual improvement will make you an effective test-taker, and working on only a few at a time will allow you to feel that these problems are solvable and that you can meet your goals.

6. **What test preparation and test-taking strategies worked best for you?** Review how you prepared and answered the test questions. Knowing what worked best enables you to repeat your success.

7. **How will you improve your test performance on the next test?** Be very specific about what you will do. Don't say, "I'll study harder." Instead, say, "I'll begin studying three

EXERCISE 9.7

ANALYZING YOUR TEST-TAKING HABITS

Be your own test coach. Analyze a test you've taken recently. Identify three major problems you had or three areas you choose to improve. Write a specific plan to eliminate the problems or improve a test-taking behavior. Then, do it.

days earlier, study a hour a day, group information to be learned, and make mnemonics to help me remember chunks of material."

If you spend some time analyzing each test, you'll discover some specific things you can do to improve your test-taking ability and your test scores. In addition, such analysis will familiarize you with test structure, making tests more familiar and less scary.

EDUCATED GUESSING TECHNIQUES

Educated guessing techniques involve using logic, reasoning, subject knowledge, and knowledge of test structure to improve your odds of guessing the correct answer on objective test questions. Be forewarned. This is a controversial topic. Some people equate the use of such techniques with cheating and claim it sullies the purity of exams. Others believe that applying educated guessing techniques is a demonstration of one's ability to think and reason. We believe that you need to learn not only the subject matter of your courses but also ways to improve your test performance. Test scores reflect both subject knowledge and test-taking ability. Educated guessing is merely one part of effective test-taking.

EXERCISE 9.8

THINKING ABOUT TESTS

Think about or discuss with others how you regard tests. Do you consider tests to be the ultimate evaluation of what you know or just one part of the learning process? How does your attitude affect how you react to taking tests and guessing on them? Do you regard educated guessing on tests to be unethical?

Educated guessing techniques are no substitute for subject mastery. Nor do they guarantee arriving at the correct answer. But, they do improve the odds of your finding the designated correct answer on an objective test question. Indeed, statisticians argue that if you work through an objective test without reading the questions and simply guess at the answers, you'll get an average of 16 percent correct.[3] And applying educated guessing techniques should increase your ability to guess well above that level. The techniques also give you a strategy to use when you simply don't know the answer to a few test questions. However, remember that nothing replaces learning the course material. Combine educated guessing techniques with your knowledge of the subject to become a more confident and proficient test-taker.

Clues to Incorrect Responses

Note: Answers to the sample questions are given at the end of the chapter on p. 161.

1. Identical Meanings If two responses are worded differently but mean or say the same thing, then neither will be the correct answer if the multiple-choice question requires you to choose the one correct answer.

1. Remembering how a clock works is an example of
   a. procedural memory
   b. your ability to remember how to do something
   c. episodic memory
   d. semantic memory[4]

If you remember that procedural memory is the ability to remember how to perform a skill or do something, then you can infer that neither *a* nor *b* is the correct answer, leaving *c* or *d* to choose from.

2. Odd or extreme choice If one response is very different from or does not easily group with other answers, then eliminate it.

2. The body's own uninfected cells are ignored by its lymphocytes because they bear _____ at their surface.
   a. complement proteins
   b. self-MHC markers
   c. antigens
   d. antigen plus self-MHC marker[5]

Answers *b, c,* and *d* all deal with antigens or self-MHC markers while *a* is the only response that contains complement proteins. Therefore, *a* is probably not the answer. When guessing, it would be better to choose from *b, c,* or *d.*

3. Joke If one response seems to be a joke, treat it as such. Test-makers get bored, and it's often a test of your knowledge to get the joke.

3. You must give a 10-minute speech to your communications class in which there are 200 students, and you are nervous. How could you inoculate yourself to reduce the stress?
   a. practice a relaxation technique
   b. practice your speech before a few friends
   c. talk to your roommate about how nervous you are
   d. get a shot[6]

Eliminate *d* and then think about what types of stress management choices *a, b,* and *c* are examples of. To do this reasoning, you need to have learned about such stress management techniques as relaxation training, inoculation technique, and social support. The question demonstrates why it is critical to learn subject vocabulary, especially in an introductory course.

4. Nonanswers Be wary of responses that state zero (0) or none of the above. It's difficult enough to write good test questions without omitting the correct answer. Much of the time a "None of the above" answer choice is not the correct answer.

4. According to Instructor Horton, goals should be set
   a. at the desired level of achievement
   b. slightly lower than the desired level of achievement so you won't be disappointed if you don't make your goal
   c. slightly higher than the desired level of achievement
   d. at the highest level to motivate you to work hard
   e. None of the above

5. True-false technique As you'll recall, absolutes are words or ways of phrasing statements so that they state or imply that the subject in question is either always or never something. Objective test responses that contain absolutes have a 99 percent probability of being false unless the subject you are being tested in is one of the natural or hard sciences (for example, physics, biology, chemistry, zoology, math, and so on). The following true-false items are all false because they contain absolutes, stated or implied.

All rapists were abused as children.

It is *only* date rape if the woman perceives it as such.[7]

[*All*] convicted rapists have a long history of hostility and violence toward both men and women.

[*All*] married couples, 40–65, who did not complete high school earn family income less than $10,000.[8]

Similarly, note the absolutes in this multiple-choice item.

5. Pollutants disrupt ecosystems because
   a. they are composed of elements that differ from those of natural molecules
   b. of all the kinds of living things, *only* humans have uses for them
   c. ecosystems have not encountered them before and so do not have any evolved mechanisms that can handle them
   d. their *only* effect is on ecosystems but not humans[9]

You should be leery of both *b* and *d* because of the stated absolutes. If you simply don't know the answer, then the best guesses would be *a* or *c*.

Clues to Potentially Correct Responses

6. Similar phrases When two responses are phrased similarly or express similar ideas, chances are one of the two is the correct answer.

6. In some societies, weaker subordinate animals may gain benefits by
   a. consistently playing the signaler role
   b. defending the group against predators rather than reproducing
   c. deferring reproduction but enjoying advantages of group living
   d. consistently being exploited by others in the group[10]

Options *b* and *c* both focus on reproduction and group belongingness, so both might be the correct answer. Also, when thinking about *b* and *c*, consider that the question asks how weaker, subordinate animals may gain benefits.

7. Opposite ideas When two responses contain opposite meanings, such as an increase and decrease in something, one of the two is probably the correct answer.

7. If the axons and dendrites of a neuron increase their branching, this will result in
   a. an increase in the number of synapses
   b. a decrease in the number of synapses
   c. the diffusion of neurotransmitter molecules
   d. the opening of the synaptic vesicles
   e. the movement of neurotransmitter molecules to the postsynaptic neuron[11]

Options *a* and *b* state opposite ideas. Often, test-writers compose an answer choice that is the exact opposite of the correct answer. Therefore, whenever you see two answer choices that state opposite ideas, consider both choices very carefully. If you haven't a clue as to what the correct answer is, guess one of the two opposites.

8. Length Often the longest answer is the best choice since it takes more words to explain something correctly, completely, and clearly than it does to state it incorrectly.

8. State-dependent memory is defined as a memory that
   a. is easiest recalled in the same environment it was formed in
   b. lasts forever

c. forms instantaneously but lasts only as long as the person pays attention

d. is easiest recalled in the same physiological state the person was in when the memory was formed[12]

Assume that you have totally blanked out on the meaning of state-dependent memory. You eliminate *b* because it is extremely short. Answers *a* and *d* refer to similar conditions while *c* contains a different idea, so you eliminate *c* and focus on *a* and *d* as the two best guesses.

9. Middle value When the answers consist of numbers, put them in numerical order and select as an answer a number from the middle of the sequence. If the answers are already in numerical order, choose from the middle answer positions—*b* or *c* if there are four choices and *b*, *c*, and *d* if there are five possible answers.

9. Children start using language in original ways at what age?
   a. $1-1\frac{1}{2}$ years
   b. $1\frac{1}{2}-2$ years
   c. $2-2\frac{1}{2}$ years
   d. $2\frac{1}{2}-3$ years[13]

Here your best guess would be *b* or *c*.

10. Repetition When answer options repeat terms, the correct answer often is the one containing the most repeated parts.

10. The atoms of certain elements are more abundant in cell structure than others. They are
    a. carbon, nitrogen, calcium, and oxygen
    b. carbon, oxygen, hydrogen, and nitrogen
    c. carbon, oxygen, hydrogen, and magnesium
    d. carbon, nitrogen, iron, and oxygen[14]

Count how many times each element appears in all four answer choices and choose the answer that contains all or most of the repeated items. In this case *b* would be a good guess.

11. Split pairs This type of question involves answer choices with two or more parts. A quick and easy way for test-writers to create incorrect but correct-looking answer choices is to combine a correct answer part with an incorrect one. Note which parts of answers are repeated in the answer choices, and choose the answer that combines the most repeated parts.

11. Cell membranes consist largely of a
    a. carbohydrate bilayer and proteins
    b. protein bilayer and phospholipids
    c. phospholipid bilayer and proteins
    d. nucleic acid bilayer and proteins[15]

Protein appears alone or in combination in each answer choice while *phospholipids* appears in two. There is a high probability that the correct answer will contain both *protein* and *phospholipid*, which eliminates *a* and *d*.

12. Vocabulary This is always a clue or aid in test-taking. Compare terms used in the question stem with synonyms in answer choices to pinpoint the probable correct answer.

12. _____ is the movement of a solute down its concentration gradient.
    a. osmosis
    b. active transport
    c. diffusion
    d. facilitated diffusion[16]

The question asks for the term that means something becoming less concentrated. The best guesses are either *c* or *d* because they both contain the term *diffusion*, which means "to spread out" or "to scatter."

13. "All of the above" answers If "all of the above" appears often as an answer choice, then it is no better a guess than any other answer. However, if it appears seldom, then the probability is high that it is the correct answer. Carefully read the answer choices. If two or more of the answer choices seem to be correct, select "all of the above."

13. Ways to predict potential test questions include paying attention to
    a. how the lecturer states information during the lecture
    b. the instructor's questions to students in class
    c. material from the text that is covered in depth in class
    d. quiz questions and homework assignments
    e. all of the above

14. Umbrella answers Test-writers often scatter parts of answers through other answer choices. It's wiser to choose the answer that includes all the pieces or the one with the most pieces.

14. Populations grow exponentially when
    a. birth rate remains above death rate and neither changes
    b. death rate remains above birth rate
    c. immigration and emigration rates are equal (a zero value)
    d. emigration rates exceed immigration rates
    e. both *a* and *c* combined are correct[17]

Options *b* and *d* seem to contradict the statement, but *a* and *c* make sense; so *e* would be your best guess.

15. Grammar Sometimes grammar clues you in to the correct answer (for example, subject-verb agreement, use of *a* versus *an*, and so on). However, both teacher-made and standardized tests can easily eliminate one type of grammatical clue by using *a(n)*.

15. Electrons are shared in a(n) _____ bond.
    a. covalent
    b. ionic
    c. hydrogen
    d. double ionic[18]

If the test-writer had written "Electrons are shared in a _____ bond," then answer *b* could have been eliminated because it is grammatically incorrect.

16. Pattern answers Test-writers tend to have answer preferences. After an objective test count the number of correct *a, b, c, d,* and *e* responses. If there's time during a test,

EXERCISE 9.9

WORKING WITH EDUCATED GUESSING CLUES

Write some objective test questions containing educated guessing clues for an upcoming test. Exchange these with a classmate or a group of students. Practice identifying the educated guessing clues as well as answering the questions. Doing this will help you learn the material and think like an instructor.

Alternative activity: When analyzing a test (refer to the section on test analysis earlier in the chapter), identify some of the educated guessing clues.

count the answers you are certain are right to see if your instructor has a preference for one position. If she or he does, then use that answer preference when guessing. If no pattern is evident, however, don't repeat the same answer letters one after another. Also, if no pattern is evident, choose T, T, F for true-false questions and *b* or *c* on multiple-choice questions.

Educated Guessing Test

1. The RNA molecules are _____
   a. a double helix
   b. usually a double nucleotide strand
   c. always a double nucleotide strand
   d. usually a single nucleotide strand[19]
2. The Public/Periodical Serials List (PSL) is a(n) _____
   a. important part of the *Library of Congress Subject Headings* reference
   b. guide to periodicals once subscribed to by the library
   c. guide to periodicals currently subscribed to by the library
   d. guide to periodicals both once and currently subscribed to by the library
   e. outline of breakfast foods
3. A feeding relationship that proceeds from algae to a fish, then to a fisherman, and finally to a shark is best described as _____
   a. a food chain
   b. a food web
   c. bad luck for the fisherman
   d. both *a* and *b*[20]
4. In a family with no daughters and two sons, the chances that the next child would be a daughter are _____
   a. 1/2
   b. 1/3
   c. 2/6
   d. 3/9
5. Two homologous chromosomes generally contain the same _____
   a. genes in reverse order
   b. alleles in the reverse order
   c. alleles in the same order
   d. none of the above[21]
6. A person has suffered damage to the cerebral cortex and has impaired perception of the left half of the body and a tendency to ignore the left half

of the body and the left half of the world. What is the probable location of the damage to the cerebral cortex?

a. the motor cortex in the left frontal lobe
b. the right occipital lobe
c. the right parietal lobe
d. the left parietal lobe
e. one of the temporal lobes[22]

7. In 1953 the United States had _____ states.

a. 47
b. 50
c. 48
d. 45

8. In response to solute concentration gradients or pressure gradients, water moves across a membrane by _____

a. osmosis
b. active transport
c. diffusion
d. facilitated diffusion

9. The passive movement of a substance through channel proteins as it follows its concentration gradient across a cell membrane is called _____

a. osmosis
b. active transport
c. diffusion
d. facilitated diffusion

10. The energy-assisted movement of a substance through transport proteins that span the cell membrane is called _____

a. osmosis
b. active transport
c. diffusion
d. facilitated diffusion

11. _____ is the movement of a solute down its concentration gradient.

a. osmosis
b. active transport
c. diffusion
d. facilitated diffusion[23]

Answers to Exercise 9.4—Matching Questions

1. e
2. b
3. d
4. f
5. c
6. g
7. a

Answers to Educated Guessing Examples

1. d
2. b
3. b
4. c
5. c
6. c
7. a
8. d
9. b
10. b
11. c
12. c
13. e
14. e
15. a

Answers to Exercise 9.10—Educated Guessing Test

1. Eliminate *c*, which contains the absolute "always," and *a*, which is an extreme answer. The correct answer is *d*.
2. Eliminate the joke answer *e*. The longest and umbrella answer *d* is correct.
3. Eliminate the joke answer *c*. Choose answer *d*, because both *a* and *b* contain "food."
4. If you don't let the numbers panic you (which is a relatively common reaction to numbers), then you'll realize that *b, c,* and *d* all mean the same thing. Thus, choose *a*.
5. Toss out the nonanswer *d*, and focus on opposite answers *b* and *c*. If you guess *b* because of the repetition of "reverse order" in both *a* and *b*, you'll be wrong. The correct answer is *c*.
6. Your two best choices would be *c* and *d* because these two answer choices both deal with the parietal lobe while the other choices deal with three different lobes. Answer *c* might be the better guess because of the repetition of "right" in both *b* and *c*. In fact, the correct answer is *c*.
7. Often you'll see this type of question with the answers given in proper numerical sequence. However, if the answers aren't in sequence, reorder them and select from the numbers in the middle of the sequence. In this example, your choices are *a* and *c*, and *c* is correct.
8. a   9. d   10. b   11. c

First, notice that the answer choices for questions 8–11 are identical and that they all focus on biological vocabulary. If you haven't learned the precise meanings of *osmosis, diffusion, active transport,* and *facilitated diffusion,* you'll likely have trouble with most or all of these questions. This is a perfect example of why studying subject vocabulary is so important.

Chances are that each answer choice is correct for one of the four questions. This is a very effective way for instructors to write good multiple-choice questions that test a student's knowledge of subject vocabulary. However, paying attention to vocabulary in both the questions and the answer choices improves your odds of guessing correctly.

Question 9 asks for the name of the "passive movement" while question 10 specifies "energy-assisted movement." Therefore, for question 9 select *d* (facilitated diffusion), which corresponds more closely to passive movement, and for question 10 choose *b* (active transport), which seems similar to energy-assisted movement. Question 11 is about a solute's downward movement. Since *diffusion* means "to spread out" or, in one sense, "to dilute or make less of," then you might equate the downward movement with simple diffusion (answer *c*).

Question 8 contains no educated guessing clues that will enable you to guess the correct answer if you have only this one question. If you are trying to answer question 8 in conjunction with questions 9–11, you could reason that, since you've used answer choices *b, c,* and *d,* the answer must be *a*—which it is. However, without the other questions for comparison, if you apply educated guessing techniques you might decide erroneously that *c* or *d* is the best choice because of similar terms. Remember, educated guessing techniques don't guarantee a correct answer; they only increase your odds of getting the right answer.

Notes

[1]Cecie Starr, *Biology: Concepts and Applications* (Belmont, CA: Wadsworth, 1991), p. 505.

[2]James W. Kalat, *Introduction to Psychology*, 2nd ed. (Belmont, CA: Wadsworth, 1990), p. 17.

[3]Michael Donner, *How to Beat the SAT* (New York: Workman, 1981).

[4]Kalat, p. 292.

[5]Starr, p. 405.

[6]Kalat, pp. 453–457 and 463.

[7]Rodney Stark, *Sociology*, 3rd ed. (Belmont, CA: Wadsworth, 1989), p. 484.

[8]Stark, p. 484.

[9]Starr, p. 585.
[10]Starr, p. 599.
[11]Kalat, pp. 70 and 97.
[12]Kalat, pp. 311–312.
[13]Kalat, pp. 209–211.
[14]Starr, p. 36.
[15]Starr, p. 57.
[16]Starr, p. 57.
[17]Starr, p. 505.
[18]Starr, p. 36.
[19]Starr, p. 162.
[20]Starr, p. 541.
[21]Starr, p. 116.
[22]Kalat, p. 86 and 97.
[23]Starr, p. 57.

WRITING ESSAY EXAMS

Tips

1. Read and follow all test directions.
2. Survey the test.
3. Pay attention to how many questions you must answer, whether you have choices of questions to answer, and how much questions are worth.
4. Plan how much time to spend on each essay question based on each question's point value.
5. Critically analyze each essay question to determine exactly what you are being asked.
6. Make a "quickplan" of main points and supporting details for your essay answer.
7. Write your essay answer in neat, easy-to-read handwriting using a blue or black ink pen.
8. Make your essay answers look professional.
9. Use correct grammar and spelling, and make needed corrections neatly.

A Left-Brained Overview

I. Good Beginnings
   A. Read test directions
   B. Choose questions you can answer most completely
   C. Jot down any ideas for answers
   D. Answer the question asked
   E. Use standard spelling and grammar
   F. Correct errors neatly
II. Steps for Planning and Writing Effective Essays
   A. Analyzing the questions
      1. Find the direction word
      2. Identify the general subject
      3. Note any restrictions—who, what, when, where
      4. Mark any specific focus or directions
   B. Making a "quickplan"
      1. Begin with three answers to the questions
      2. Add supporting or clarifying points to each answer
   C. Writing the answer
      1. Begin with an introductory statement
      2. Develop each main point in the body
      3. End with a concluding statement
III. When the Test is Returned
   A. Read the instructor's comments
   B. Look for the essay's strong and weak points

A Right-Brained Overview

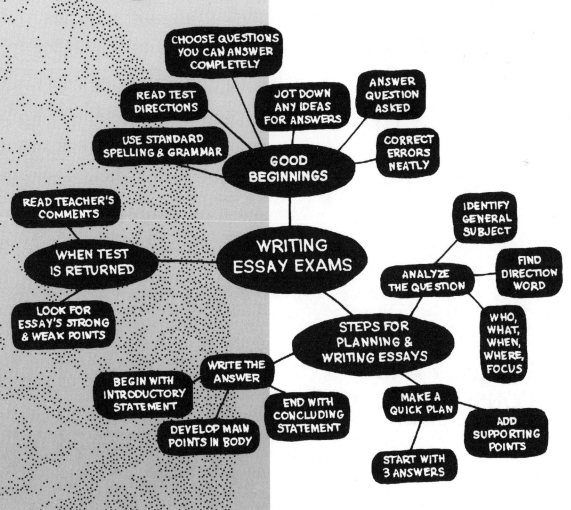

CHOOSE QUESTIONS YOU CAN ANSWER COMPLETELY

READ TEST DIRECTIONS

JOT DOWN ANY IDEAS FOR ANSWERS

ANSWER QUESTION ASKED

USE STANDARD SPELLING & GRAMMAR

CORRECT ERRORS NEATLY

GOOD BEGINNINGS

READ TEACHER'S COMMENTS

WHEN TEST IS RETURNED

WRITING ESSAY EXAMS

IDENTIFY GENERAL SUBJECT

ANALYZE THE QUESTION

FIND DIRECTION WORD

LOOK FOR ESSAY'S STRONG & WEAK POINTS

STEPS FOR PLANNING & WRITING ESSAYS

WHO, WHAT, WHEN, WHERE, FOCUS

WRITE THE ANSWER

BEGIN WITH INTRODUCTORY STATEMENT

END WITH CONCLUDING STATEMENT

MAKE A QUICK PLAN

ADD SUPPORTING POINTS

DEVELOP MAIN POINTS IN BODY

START WITH 3 ANSWERS

You've worked hard all semester but you're nervous about the big essay exam coming up. You're afraid that you'll panic and forget everything you've learned. Or perhaps you're simply concerned that you won't be able to craft coherent essays under exam conditions. In this chapter we'll give you a step-by-step system for writing essay exams.

IS THIS YOU?

GOOD BEGINNINGS

Imagine that you're taking an environmental science course and your instructor gives you the following essay exam. How would you proceed?

ECOLOGY AND CONSERVATION EXAM[1]

General Instructions: Answer a total of four (4) questions using the blue books provided by the test proctors. If you need additional blue books, request them from a proctor. Write in pen. Make any corrections neatly. Put your test ID number only on the front of each blue book. Do not put your name on the blue books. Total test point value: 100. Total test time: 1 hour and 30 minutes.

I. Answer one (1) of the following. Value: 10 points.

1. List ten of the most important things an individual can do to save energy in the home and in transportation.

2. List ten prevention strategies that a person can use to reduce personal risks from various hazards.

3. Name the common physical, chemical, and biological hazards that people face and explain the effects of each.

II. Answer one (1) of the following. Value: 15 points.

1. In a sentence name, define, and give the major symptoms of the major types of STDs. Briefly explain ways to reduce the risks of being infected with an STD.

2. Name and define the major types and sources of air pollutants.

3. What are the major advantages and disadvantages of using insecticides and herbicides?

III. Answer one (1) of the following. Value: 25 points.

1. Explain how a river can cleanse itself of oxygen-demanding wastes. Comment on what helps a river successfully cleanse itself and what can cause the river to fail to clean itself.

2. Choose one of the listed options and discuss the advantages and disadvantages of using that energy source for some or all of the United States' energy needs.

  a. sun's direct input of solar energy
  b. indirect solar energy stored in falling and flowing water
  c. indirect solar energy stored in winds
  d. renewable, indirect solar energy stored in plants and organic waste
  e. producing and using hydrogen gas and fuel cells

3. Choose one of the listed sources of energy. Discuss its uses, advantages, and disadvantages as an energy resource.

  a. oil
  b. natural gas
  c. coal
  d. geothermal energy
  e. nuclear fission (conventional and breeder) and nuclear fusion

IV. Answer one (1) of the following questions. Agree or disagree with the statement and support your point of view. Value: 50 points.

1. Should a heavy federal tax be placed on gasoline and imported oil used in the U.S.?

2. Should all smoking be banned in public buildings and commercial airplanes, buses, subways, and trains?

3. Should most of society's wastes be dumped in the ocean because it is a vast sink for diluting, dispersing, and degrading wastes?

4. Should U.S. companies continue to be allowed to export pesticides, medicines, and other chemicals that have been banned or severely restricted in the United States to other countries?

1. **Read the test directions first, noting question options and point values, and plan your test time**. The limited amount of test time is a real killer on an essay test. You need to plan adequate time to write essay answers that are long enough and contain enough detail. Divide your test time according to how many points each essay question is worth. If a question is worth half of the entire test, then give it half the test time available. Suppose the sample ecology and conservation test was a 90-minute affair. Deducting 10 minutes for the instructor to pass out the exam and answer questions and for you to read the directions, your time budget might look like this:

50-point essay	40 minutes
25-point essay	20 minutes
15-point essay	10 minutes
10-point essay	5 minutes
TOTAL TIME	75 minutes

In the remaining 5 minutes you could review your essays.

2. **Choose the questions you can answer most completely in the least amount of time**. A test is a performance rated by your final grade. Choosing to answer a fascinating, thought-provoking question instead of one requiring you to regurgitate basic information may result in your losing precious test time. Save the fascinating questions for class discussions.

3. **As you first read the exam jot down any ideas and possible answers on the test**. This frees you from having to remember them later. Write just enough to jog your memory; don't waste valuable test time writing complete sentences or a formal outline at this point.

The United States' ~~excessive use~~ *excessive use* of oil *and* gasoline

The United States' ~~excesive~~ *excessive* use of oil *and* gasoline contributes

Figure 10.1
Sloppy Versus Neat Corrections

4. **Answer the question asked**. A major reason students lose points on essay exams is that they do not answer the exact question asked. Instead, they write about the subject in general. If you've ever had a teacher write, "You are correct in what you say, but you didn't answer my question," then you've written around the question. This doesn't get you any test points. To make sure you are giving the asked-for information, analyze the question before you begin to write. See the section later in this chapter for information on how to analyze an essay question.

5. **Use standard grammar and spelling**. These count. Many instructors will lower the grade of a knowledgeable essay answer if it has grammatical and spelling errors.

6. **Correct errors neatly**. It's much better to correct a mistake than to leave it, hoping the instructor won't notice. Figure 10.1 shows examples of neat and messy corrections.

STEPS FOR PLANNING AND WRITING EFFECTIVE ESSAYS

Good essays don't just appear on the page. Rather, they result from a three-step process: (1) analyzing the question, (2) making a "quickplan," and only then (3) writing.

I. Analyzing the Questions

Before you begin writing or even outlining your essay, you need to read the question carefully to locate the following:

- The direction word
- The general subject of the question
- Any who, what, when, and where restrictions
- Any specific focus or special directions

Direction words tell you what kind of essay you're being asked to write. Direction words come in several types:
- *Identification:* This is the least complex essay type and often involves the shortest answer. Identification requires explaining *who* and/or *what* the person or

event is, *when* and *where* the person lived or the event occurred, and *how* or *why* the person or event was significant. These essay answers must be specific. An excellent technique for writing answers for these types of questions is to write a sentence or two using the FITS format (see Chapter 6). Typical identification words include the following:

cite	indicate	state	list
give	identify	define	enumerate
name			

- **Description:** This essay type involves providing the information one would for an identification-type essay plus enough details to create a picture with words. Thus, specific, concrete examples, facts, proof, or other supporting information is required. The length of the essay depends on the number of points; the more points, the longer the essay needs to be. Typical description words include the following:

give	develop	discuss	summarize
diagram	outline	sketch	trace
illustrate	describe	review	

- **Relation:** This essay type involves providing the type of information required in both identification and description essays plus showing a connection or association between two or more terms, ideas, people, events, and so on. These direction words usually appear in the higher-point-value questions and require you to demonstrate thinking about the subject, not just recite facts from memory. Typical relation words include the following:

analyze	compare	contrast	differentiate
distinguish	relate		

- **Demonstration:** This essay type requires using the techniques of identification and description and possibly relation questions as well as using details and examples to show why an idea or conclusion is true or false. The focus of this type of essay is on using facts, information, concepts, and ideas to demonstrate critical thinking about the subject. These are almost always longer, higher-point-value essay questions. Typical demonstration words include the following:

demonstrate   explain   justify   prove

support

- ***Evaluation:*** This essay type is the most complex and most demanding. Not only must you use the techniques of identification and description, you must also apply the techniques of demonstration. In addition, you must make a judgment about the point in question, provide concrete support for that judgment, and show the reasoning process necessary to arrive at or support that judgment. Typical evaluation words include the following:

assess   comment   criticize   evaluate

interpret   propose

Here are some questions from the sample ecology and conservation essay exam that have been analyzed. Note that in each case, in addition to finding the direction words, we locate both the general subject and the specific focus and pinpoint any who, what, when, and where restrictions.

Question 1:

DIRECTION WORD   Specific Focus   WHO
List ten of the most important things an individual can do

   GENERAL SUBJECT
     OR WHAT   WHERE
to save energy in the home and in transportation.

Question 2:

        DIRECTION WORDS   WHAT
In a sentence name, define, and give the major symptoms

                 Direction
     general subject   word   specific focus
of the major types of STDs. Briefly explain one or two ways

   general subject   WHAT
to reduce the risks of being infected with an STD.

Question 3:

   WHAT   general subject
A heavy federal tax should be placed on gasoline and im-

       WHERE
ported oil used in the U.S.

Note that in the last case the general instructions for this section said to agree or disagree with the statement and to support it. Therefore, the direction word is *support*.

2. Making a "Quickplan"

After analyzing the question, you'll want to create a "quickplan" on which to base your answer. First, jot down three points or ideas to answer the question. You can write this in traditional left-brained outline form or in a right-brained spidergram form (see Chapter 5 for instructions on how to create a spidergram). Next, add details to support or clarify each of the three major points generated in step 1. For example, suppose you created a quickplan to outline the 50-point essay question "A heavy federal tax should be placed on gasoline and imported oil used in the U.S." Figure 10.2 shows a left-brained quickplan showing the three main points and supporting details for the argument that a federal tax should be imposed. Figure 10.3 shows the same information written in the form of a right-brained quickplan. When creating a quickplan, aim for three supporting details for each main point. However, if you can think of only two, that's much better than one or none. If you need to write a longer essay answer, simply add three more details to each of the supporting details. Continue this process as long as necessary.

Before writing your essay answer, look over your quickplan to check that the details logically support the point and that supporting points answer the question asked. Decide on the order in which you'll discuss the supporting points. We recommend that you begin with

1. To shift dependence on oil
   - U.S. uses 30% of all oil extracted in world
   - 2/3 of world's oil reserves in OPEC countries
   - 40% of U.S. oil imported
   - U.S. uses 2/3 of its oil for transportation
   - dependence on foreign oil skews u.S. economy and world political position

2. To reduce environmental pollution
   - Fossil fuel burning=air & water pollution
   - Less use of petrol products reduces other types pollution—pesticides, plastics
   - Disposal problem result of so many cars

3. Crude oil supply limited
   - Estimated world oil reserves will last 33 yrs; U.S. reserves empty 2005
   - Oil extraction methods get only 1/3 of crude; expensive to recover other

Figure 10.2
Sample Left-Brained Quickplan

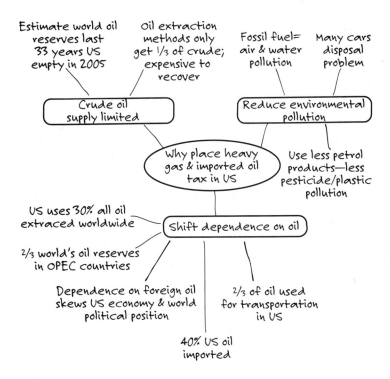

Figure 10.3
Sample Right-Brained Quickplan

EXERCISE 10.3

USING QUICKPLANS

Write an essay question for one of your classes. Analyze it and make a quickplan. If you learn best by talking things over, do this exercise by talking through it with a group of students from your class.

Alternative activity: Exchange an essay question you've written with someone else in the class. Analyze and make a quickplan for their question while they do the same with yours.

the point with the least amount of information and end strongly by discussing the point about which you have the most information.

3. Writing the Answers

When you write your actual essay answers, use the same standard prose organization form, whether the essay is one paragraph long or several. Begin with an introductory sentence that restates the main subject of the essay question and gives the major points your essay answer will discuss. Remember to list the major points you'll discuss in the order you will discuss them. Consider again the sample essay item "A heavy federal tax should be placed on gasoline and imported oil used in the U.S." Look at how the following introductory sentence uses part of the essay question, states that the essay will argue in favor of such a tax, and then lists three reasons for being in favor of such a tax.

A heavy federal tax should be placed on gasoline and oil used in the U.S. because such a tax would help reduce environmental pollution, preserve the limited supply of crude oil, and shift U.S. dependence on foreign oil.

Next, develop each of your main points. You may require only a few sentences to explain each major point, or you may need to write a paragraph or more for each one. How much you write depends on the point value of the essay: the more points, the longer the essay discussion needs to be. Notice the development of the main points of our sample essay; the main points are underlined.

Oil and gasoline use contribute greatly to air, water, and land pollution in the United States. A primary contributor to pollution is the automobile, which consumes approximately two-thirds of the total U.S. oil use. That burning of oil and gasoline results in 50 percent of the air pollution. Water is polluted by oil and gasoline spills occurring while fuel is being produced for transportation use. Further water pollution results from the dumping of engine oil. Transportation contributes to land pollution through the large-scale use of land for roads, parking spaces, and ultimately places to discard worn-out cars. A federal tax on oil and gasoline would make it more expensive to operate automobiles causing many people to begin using other forms of transportation and leading to the development of different types of fuels to power the automobile. This would result in less use of oil and gasoline with a secondary effect being less air, water, and land pollution caused by fossil-fuel-burning forms of transportation.

A second reason for imposing a heavy federal tax on oil and gasoline is to preserve the limited supply of crude oil. Experts estimate that world crude oil reserves will last only another 33 years while at current consumption rates U.S. oil reserves will be depleted very early in the twenty-first century. Although about two-thirds of crude oil is left in a well by current drilling methods, it's costly to recover the remaining oil and to refine that type of crude oil. By focusing only on producing oil to maintain current consumption, we continue to add to environmental pollution, to increase prices of transportation, and to deplete oil reserves. A heavy federal tax on oil and gasoline would result in a reduction of oil and gasoline for transportation use, preserving both the environment and the dwindling oil supplies. This would give us additional time to develop more efficient fuels and transportation systems.

The United States' massive use of oil and gasoline results in a critical dependence on foreign sources for crude oil. This causes problems for the U.S. economy and skews our world political position. The U.S. uses 30 percent of the world's oil supply but imports 40 percent of all the oil used. Since two-thirds of the world's oil supplies are in the Middle East and controlled by OPEC countries, the U.S. is vulnerable both economically and politically because of our dependence on foreign oil. A heavy federal tax would begin to shift U.S. oil use and lessen our dependence on foreign supplies.[2]

Finally, conclude the essay with a sentence or a paragraph, depending on the length of the essay. Sum up your argument or draw conclusions about what you've already discussed, or restate your main points. Do not just stop writing. Let your reader know that you really were finished. Here is the conclusion of the sample essay:

> The United States' excessive use of oil and gasoline contributes greatly to pollution, uses up a nonrenewable energy resource, and forces the U.S. to rely on foreign oil supplies. A heavy federal tax imposed on oil and gasoline would decrease oil and gasoline use and reduce air, water, and land pollution. The tax would increase oil and gasoline costs, making discovery of more efficient and cheaper fuels attractive. The U.S. would become less dependent on foreign oil sources. These are some of the reasons I favor imposing a heavy federal tax on oil and gasoline used in the U.S.

Don't waste your valuable test time trying to dazzle your instructor with your prose. Just keep your essay answer organized, clear, and well supported.

WHEN THE TEST IS RETURNED

Of course, you'll look at the grade first. But do more than that. Read the instructor's comments. What were the essay's weaknesses and strengths? What did you do right and where did you miss the boat? Pay attention to the good and the bad. You can learn from both. Take a look at the process for evaluating your test performance on an objective test in Chapter 9. It might give you some additional points to consider. Discuss your essay with a friend or your instructor. Write down one or two ways you'll improve your essay writing performance on the next test. Then, do them. If you do this after each essay exam, soon you'll be a champion essay test-taker.

Notes

[1]Test questions and answer information taken from G. Tyler Miller, Jr., *Living in the Environment: An Introduction to Environmental Science*, 6th ed. (Belmont, CA: Wadsworth, 1990), Chapters 17–22.

[2]Information used to write the sample essay based on Miller, *Living in the Environment*, pp. 375–382.

Epilogue: What Next?

to educate, *vt*, to develop mentally, morally, or aesthetically; to persuade or condition to feel, believe, or act in a desired way or to accept something as desirable.
Webster's Ninth New Collegiate Dictionary

Congratulations! You have now finished reading this text. Perhaps you have completed your freshman seminar class and/or first year of college. Now what? Where do you go from here?

Your education will not stop when you earn that coveted degree or diploma. Your education will continue as long as you are alive. You have just laid the foundation for continuing and celebrating lifelong learning. Education is a process, not a goal.

There are at least two, separate and distinct objectives of higher education. Too often students focus only on the first, which is earning enough credits to get a desired degree. Later, the value of the second objective—that of obtaining knowledge—becomes more and more apparent. We encourage you to strive to succeed to attain both objectives. Don't just focus on earning enough credits or getting specific training to do one specific job. Expand your mind, your learning, and your horizons during this special time in your life.

The skills and tips in this book will enable you to be a lifelong, independent learner. As you grow and change, you will need continually to hone these skills and abilities and to revise your plans and strategies accordingly.

We encourage you always to add more experiential knowledge to the foundation you have laid. As you complete this, the first step of your journey, we congratulate you and, as we did at the start of this book, we wish you *bon voyage*!
Nancy L. Matte and Sue Henderson

Appendix A

Writing Assignments

I. TYPICAL WRITING ASSIGNMENTS

Critique: Also called an *evaluation, critical essay,* or *opinion paper*; primarily a rational and considered reaction to some form of communication (book, story, film, article, and so on). In a critique the writer provides a brief summary of the content of the work in question. The bulk of the critique is comprised of the writer's considered opinion as to the work's purpose, validity, worth, and overall quality. This opinion is supported and clarified by specific details. The section beginning on page 186 contains a series of open-ended questions for collecting information and organizing your critique.

Explication: A close reading and explanation of a work, usually a poem or other piece of literature, a piece of music (melody or lyrics), or a work of art. The purpose of an explication is to explain the meaning of the work by examining thematic development, structure, tone, imagery, and the experience being conveyed. The section beginning on page 187 gives detailed instructions for writing an explication.

Laboratory report: A report of work in a science class laboratory. Its purpose is threefold: as a scientific learning tool; as a way to analyze data; and as a record of the work completed and the investigative techniques used. The section beginning on page 189 gives detailed instructions on writing a laboratory report.

Letter of complaint: A letter in standard business format explaining some problem and an expected solution. Typically the first paragraph provides the basic facts and states the problem; the second paragraph goes into more detail about the problem; and the third paragraph states what the writer expects to be done to solve the problem or provide compensation.

Research paper: A typed paper, ranging from 3–5 pages in length to 25 pages or more, that presents the results of extensive research. Typically this is the major project in the second semester of first-year English composition classes, although research papers may be assigned in several other classes as well. Research papers are not necessarily difficult (though they are time-consuming) if you break down the project into manageable chunks. The section beginning on page 192 traces the steps for writing a research paper.

Resume and cover letter: A *resume* is usually a one-page information sheet listing a person's qualifications for a job to a prospective employer. Resumes require specific data presented in one of several recommended formats. Check with your college's career placement office or check out a book on resume preparation from the library. A *cover letter* accompanies the resume when one is applying for a specific job. The cover letter directs attention to information on the resume that one feels is particularly pertinent to the job in question, or it gives the prospective employer more detailed information than can be provided in the resume.

Slanting: More a method of treating material than an actual writing type; involves using factual information and language in such a way that an unbalanced or one-sided picture or idea is suggested. In many ways, slanting is a propaganda technique—for example, Hitler as German national hero, or Princess Diana as royal disgrace.

Summary: A brief recap of the main ideas of a book, movie, play, speech, and so on. The five-sentence summary format works especially well. Sentence 1 states the three main ideas of the work being summarized by answering the basic who, what, when, and where questions. Sentences 2–4 are single-sentence statements about each of the three main ideas. Sentence 5 makes a judgment, draws a conclusion, or restates the work's main point. The section beginning on page 191 gives detailed instructions on how to write a summary.

Theme or essay: A piece of writing usually assigned in English composition classes, ranging from one long paragraph to several pages in length. Its primary purpose is to have you practice organizing ideas and information in written form. Instructors may request a specific organization such as *expository* (a main idea supported by details), *narrative* (an idea explained or told in story form), *comparison and contrast* (a discussion of the similarities and differences of at least two similar items, such as football and soccer), *process* (basically, instructions on how to do something), or *cause and effect* (a look at what caused or resulted from something). Consult your English composition textbook for detailed explanations of how to write the various types. A standard organization for first-year English themes is the five-paragraph essay. Paragraph 1 introduces the topic and contains the thesis statement; paragraphs 2–4 discuss the three main points being made about the topic; paragraph 5 concludes the essay. Each individual paragraph of the essay should have a topic sentence supported by details and a concluding sentence. Of course, correct spelling, grammar, and usage are essential.

II. GUIDELINES FOR WRITING AND SPEAKING ASSIGNMENTS

1. **Know precisely what the assignment is**. For example, how long is it supposed to be? What topics can you choose from? How is it to be written (typed, handwritten, one side of the page only, and so on)? How many sources are you required to consult? How are you to document them? When is the assignment due? Exactly what is to be handed in?

2. **Choose and narrow your topic**. If any step will save you time and make writing or speaking projects less painful, this is it. The topic choice exercise on page 185 gives one method of surveying a broad subject area and narrowing the topic down. Another technique for doing this is to brainstorm your ideas using the spidergram format. If you need some background information on a topic before narrowing it down, encyclopedia articles are good sources of basic information.

Note: Spend no more than 30 minutes on this step.

3. **Collect the information you need**. Check out some books from the library. Read some articles in journals or magazines or newspapers. Interview somebody. Use your computer information service. Watch a film. Listen to a tape. If you're doing extensive research, the section beginning on page 192 outlines an effective method for collecting and organizing information before you write.

Note: How much time you spend on this step will vary, depending on how much information you need. You can break the research process down into manageable chunks by deciding that you'll go to the library, read, interview, or whatever for a specified time. For example, you may plan to go to the library for one hour on Tuesday, 30 minutes on Wednesday, and 40 minutes on Friday. By doing the research in pieces, you'll probably get better results than if you had tried to do it all at once.

4. **Make an outline**. It's best to create an outline *before* you write. Remember, outlines are plans of how you think you'll proceed; they can be changed during the writing process. Trying to write without an outline is like trying to find your destination without a road map. Eventually you may get where you were going, but you'll make a lot of wrong turns before you do.

Note: You can use the traditional, left-brained outline format, with Roman numerals and Arabic numbers and capital and lowercase letters. Or you can use the right-brained spidergram format. In either case, this step should take no more than 45 minutes.

5. **Write a thesis statement**. This is a guide to what you do and do not put into your assignment. Use the FITS formula to help yourself create an effective thesis statement. This sentence may never appear in your final work, but it will keep you properly focused.

Note: Spend only 5 or 10 minutes doing this.

6. **Write your rough draft**. You can write the whole assignment in one sitting or you can break it up into several smaller chunks of writing time. This is a rough draft, so concentrate on simply getting your ideas down on paper.

If possible, write your rough draft on a word processor. It makes the next step—revision—much easier. If you don't know how to use a word processor, now is the time to learn, in a class or on your own. If you don't own one, check whether your college has some sort of laboratory where you can use a computer; most do.

Note: How much time you spend on this step will vary greatly, depending on your assignment and your writing skills.

7. **Revise your work**. Reread your rough draft or have a friend or tutor read it to make sure it makes sense, is logical, and has enough information to support your main ideas. Check the spelling. If your word processing program has this feature, do it on the computer. If not, you'll have to do it the old fashioned way—yourself. Check the grammar as well.

Tip: If you have a problem with sentence structure, print out a hard copy and mark each period with a heavy, dark marker. Then, read aloud each chunk ending with a period. Your ears are much better than your eyes at catching grammatical errors, especially incomplete or run-on sentences. Have you said enough? Too much? Add or cut as needed. Recheck to make sure that you have included everything your instructor wants.

Warning: If you are using a computer spelling check program, at least once print out a hard copy and read through what you've written. Spell checkers only check for correct English words; they do not recognize whether the word makes sense in context. For example, consider the case of a newspaper that did a global search for the word *black*, instructing the computer to replace this with the more politically correct *African-American*. The computer produced this headline: "Economy in the African-American."

8. **Apply the finishing touches**. Staple pages together or put them in a folder if your instructor has requested that. Make sure you have a cover sheet if that was asked for. No matter what, make sure your name and page numbers are on the assignment. If you wrote the assignment by hand, don't rip pages out of a spiral notebook and turn in a paper with ragged edges. A professional-looking paper will earn you a higher grade than a sloppy paper that looks as if it were slapped together without much care.

Suggestion: Type your papers. Studies have shown that typed papers earn, on the average, one letter grade higher than the identical paper handwritten.

9. **Reward yourself**. No matter how you feel about the finished product, you've put forth the effort and deserve a reward. It doesn't have to be anything big—watching a favorite TV program, spending time with friends, going to a movie, or buying yourself something you've wanted. If you reward yourself when you complete academic tasks, you'll have more incentive to start them. As time goes on, you can delay the rewards and "save up" for bigger rewards.

III. CHOOSING AND NARROWING YOUR TOPIC

Spending some time thinking about possible topics will do more to save you both time and pain than probably any other step in the writing process. To narrow your topic, do the following:

1. **Use your assignment guidelines and brainstorm several possible topics**. You may find that it is easier and more productive to do this with a group. Figure A.1 shows the right-brained brainstorming of possible topics for a research paper.

2. **Use the topic choice exercise to narrow your topic**. After spending about 15 minutes brainstorming possible ideas, suppose you choose political speeches and styles as a general research subject. Now you need to spend another half hour or so focusing and narrowing the topic. To do this, answer the familiar questions (who? what? where? when? why? how?). Figure A.2 shows how you might record sample answers.

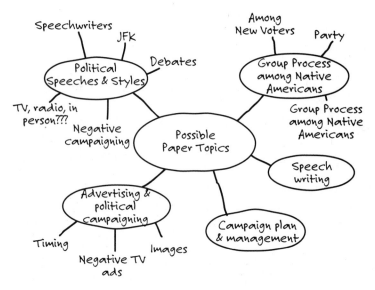

Figure A.1
Sample Right-Brained Brainstorming of Possible Topics for Research Paper

Topic: **Political Speeches & Speaking styles**

	WHO:	WHAT:	WHERE:	WHEN:	WHY:	HOW:
1.	John F. Kennedy	TV debates	U.S.	1960	Why JFK beat Nixon	Use of TV
2.	Franklin D. Roosevelt	Presidential speeches	Foreign countries	1940s	Why style is important	Image building
3.	Democrats & Republicans	Campaign speeches	in Congress	1990s	Role of content	How speaking style affects campaigns
4.	Richard Nixon	Checkers speech	California	1952	Effect of public perception	Use of TV

Figure A.2
Sample Topic Choices for Research Paper on Political Speeches and Speaking Styles

3. **Write several possible research questions**. Based on the ideas generated in step 2, choose one item from several of the categories and combine them to create a possible research question. Following are some examples of possible research topics or questions based on the more general research topic of political speeches and styles.

In 1960 how did the use of television influence the outcome of the debates between John F. Kennedy and Richard Nixon?

CHOOSING A TOPIC

Using a writing or speaking assignment, brainstorm possible topics, choose one, and complete the worksheet in Figure A.3. Then write several possible research questions or working thesis statements for the topic.

Alternative exercise: Do the same thing in a group. By doing this exercise in a group, it is possible to develop a number of different research questions or thesis statements on the same topic so that all members of the group will have a different approach for the same general topic.

In the twentieth century how did a candidate's speaking style affect how the political campaign was developed and managed? (Consider using Roosevelt, Kennedy, and Adlai Stevenson as examples.)

In the 1990s how is a political candidate's image created and projected in her or his campaign speeches?

How do a candidate's campaign speeches compare with his presidential speeches?

Now that you have several focused research questions, you can choose one to research. Make a trip to the library to check on the availability of sources and then begin creating the working bibliography (see page 192).

General research topic (before narrowing) _____

	WHO:	WHAT:	WHERE:	WHEN:	WHY:	HOW:
1.						
2.						
3.						
4.						

Figure A.3
Worksheet for Narrowing a Topic

IV. PREPARING TYPICAL WRITING ASSIGNMENTS

Writing a Critique

Bibliography Collect the following information about your subject:

1. Author or creator _____
2. Title _____
3. Part of larger work? _____
4. Publisher _____ Where _____
   When _____ Pages _____
5. Other _____

Now, rearrange this information into the standard order for a bibliography, using correct punctuation. See the *Modern Language Association Handbook*, your English Composition textbook chapter on research, William Coyle's *Research Papers*, or another book on documenting research for specific directions on how to create bibliography entries for a book, article, film, record, and so on.

Summary Collect the following information about your subject.

1. Who is the story or the work about? Give name(s).

   _____

2. Where and when does the story or work take place?

   _____

3. What are three major events of the story or messages or themes of the work?
   a. _____
   b. _____
   c. _____

Now, take this information and write it in sentence form.

Objective evaluation Answer the following questions.

1. Why are the actions being taken? *Or* Why is the creator creating this work? *Or* What idea is the creator trying to communicate?

   _____

2. What methods does the creator use to achieve her or his purpose? Give examples.

WRITING A CRITIQUE

Use the methodology just presented to write a critical essay for one of your classes. If you have no such assignment for any of your classes, try doing a critique of a movie or TV program you've seen.

a. _____
_____

b. _____
_____

c. _____
_____

3. Do each of these methods work? Why or why not? Use specific details to support your judgments.

a. _____
_____

b. _____
_____

c. _____
_____

Now, take your answers and write one or more paragraphs.

Personal reaction

1. Did you enjoy this work? _____
2. Why did you or did you not enjoy it? Give specific reasons.

a. _____
b. _____
c. _____

Writing an Explication

Suppose you were assigned to write an explication of the following poem, "Valediction: Forbidding Mourning," by seventeenth-century poet John Donne.[1]

> 1. *As virtuous men pass mildly away,*
> *And whisper to their souls to go,*
> *Whilst some of their said friends do say,*
> *"The breath goes now," and some say, "No,"*
>
> 2. *So let us melt, and make no noise,*
> *No tear-floods, nor sigh-tempests move;*
> *'Twere profanation of our joys*
> *To tell the laity our love.*
>
> 3. *Moving of the earth brings harms and fears,*
> *Men reckon what it did and meant;*
> *But trepidation of the spheres,*
> *Though greater far, is innocent.*
>
> 4. *Dull sublunary lovers' love*
> *(Whose soul is sense) cannot admit*
> *Absence, because it doth remove*
> *Those things which elemented it.*

5. But we, by a love so much refined
   That our selves know now what it is,
   Inter-assured of the mind,
   Care less, eyes, lips, and hands to miss.
6. Our two souls therefore, which are one,
   Though I must go, endure not yet
   A breach, but an expansion,
   Like gold to airy thinness beat.
7. If they be two, they are two so
   As stiff twin compasses are two:
   Thy soul, the fixed foot, makes no show
   To move, but doth, if the other do;
8. And though it in the center sit,
   Yet when the other far doth roam,
   It leans and hearkens after it,
   And grows erect, as that comes home.
9. Such wilt thou be to me, who must,
   Like the other foot, obliquely run;
   Thy firmness makes my circle just,
   And makes me end where I begun.

When you first read it, you may not be sure of what Donne is talking about, much less understand it. By answering a series of specific questions, however, you can unlock the poem's meaning. Let's apply this process to the Donne poem.

1.	**Whom is the poem about?**	A man preparing to go away.
2.	**Who is the speaker?**	The man.
3.	**Whom is the poem's speaker talking to?**	A woman, probably his lover or wife.
4.	**What is the poem about?**	How their relationship will be, even when they are separated.
5.	**When is the poem taking place?**	It doesn't say, but footnotes say it was written about 1611.
6.	**Where is the poem taking place?**	It doesn't say, but probably somewhere in England.
7.	**How is the poem structured?**	In four-line stanzas, with an *abab* rhyme scheme.

8. **What are the main actions or events of the poem?**
   a. *Stanza 1:* Something about a man dying and his friends saying yes, he's dead; no, he's not.
   b. *Stanza 2:* About being quiet, not crying, and not telling laity about love.
   c. *Stanza 3:* Something about earthquakes and spheres and harms and fears.
   d. *Stanza 4:* About changeable and earthly lovers and absence (from each other?).

WRITING AN EXPLICATION

Using the methodology just presented, write an explication on the meaning of a piece of literature, a film, a song, or a work of art.

e. *Stanza 5:* The man says their love is different.

f. *Stanza 6:* Even when the man and woman are separated, they are not apart.

g. *Stanza 7:* He says they are like "stiff twin compasses" with the woman being the "fixed foot" who moves only when the man does.

h. *Stanza 8:* Something about sitting in the center and leaning when the other one roams.

i. *Stanza 9:* About the woman being his center and returning point.

9. **What type and level of language is used?** — Formal, seventeenth-century English.

10. **What unfamiliar words are used?** — valediction, profanation, laity, sublunary, compass

11. **What images are used?**
    a. *Visual:* "gold to airy thinness beat," "twin compasses"
    b. *Auditory:* "whisper to their souls," "no tear-floods, nor sigh-temptests"
    c. *Touch:* none
    d. *Taste:* none

12. **What experience is being conveyed?** — How two people in love who are about to be separated feel.

13. **How might the main idea of the poem be summarized?** — A man leaving his lover says their love unites their souls, making them unseparable.[2]

Once you've answered the questions, it's easier to understand that Donne was writing about how this man and woman have such a strong relationship that they are part of each other even when they are physically separated. To finish the explication, define the unfamiliar terms and explain the images used. Then, present the information in standard report form.

In addition to answering the basic questions, consider the following when explicating other types of works:

point of view

major and minor characters

conflict in the story

conflict resolution

Writing a Laboratory Report

When writing a lab report, follow the general guidelines for a writing or speaking assignment outlined previously. In your lab report, be sure to do the following:

PREPARING AND EVALUATING LAB REPORTS

Write a laboratory report for one of your science classes. Then, in a group or with the entire class, sit in a circle and pass your lab report to the person sitting on your right. Read the lab report you were handed. Continue passing and reading the lab reports until everyone in the group or class has read all the lab reports. Discuss which papers were best and why. Take notes on the qualities of a good lab report.[3]

1. **State the laboratory investigation's purpose**. Use the FITS formula (discussed in Chapter 6) as a way to write a clear, concise, and brief purpose statement.

2. **Describe the investigation's procedure**. Include in this section a description or drawing of any unfamiliar equipment and methods of measurement, including what was measured and how it was measured.

3. **Present data and error analyses**. Include any raw data used to calculate results. You may find that presenting data in graph form is the most effective method. Indicate how you performed your calculations, but do not include your actual calculations. Also present the probable errors in your investigation that might affect your results. You may find it effective to list qualitative and quantitative types of possible errors.

4. **Draw a conclusion**. Discuss the assumptions on which you based your experiment, the generalizations or conclusions you can make based on the data you collected, and of the investigation's results. Generalizations need to be related closely to the experiment's purpose and supported by the data you have presented in your report. The conclusion may focus on a comparison of your results with what was expected or with others' results. Also, you may discuss the limitations of the experiment and suggest avenues of further investigation.[4]

Preparing a Speech

The initial steps for preparing a speech are very similar to the basic steps for putting together a paper: (1) know precisely what the assignment is, (2) choose and narrow your topic carefully, (3) collect the information you need, and (4) write a thesis statement. Next, make an outline of your main and supporting points, in either phrases or complete sentences. The outline should be detailed enough so that you can use it to guide your speech. You may find that writing your points on 3 × 5 cards works better than putting it on sheets of paper. You do not want to write out your speech word for word because you

PREPARING A SPEECH
Use the methodology just given to prepare a speech on a topic that interests you. If you are using this book in a college success class, your instructor may ask you to do a brief presentation on a college resource, a possible career, or a potential major.

could end up simply reading the speech. Not only can this make your delivery sound wooden, but you might lose your place. Instead, use the outline as a launching pad to jog your memory as you create the speech.

Next, practice giving your speech, either in front of a mirror or to a friend or family member. Time yourself to make sure you are meeting any time requirements. Pay attention to the flow of ideas, to distracting speech or body mannerisms, and to the tone of your voice. You may find it useful to tape your speech as you practice and to critique your presentation.

Writing a Summary

To illustrate the use of the five-sentence summary plan, let's consider Margaret Mitchell's epic novel *Gone with the Wind*. Our summarizing process might go as follows:

- **Sentence 1:** An introductory thesis or topic sentence that answers the basic who? what? when? and where? questions and presents three main ideas or events.
- **Sentences 2–4:** The body of the summary that discusses the three main ideas in detail.
- **Sentence 5:** A judgment or conclusion or restatement of the introductory sentence ideas.

Here's how our one-paragraph summary might look:

(1) Margaret Mitchell's novel *Gone with the Wind*, set primarily in Atlanta, Georgia, and on the O'Hara's plantation Tara during the 1860s, is the story of Scarlett O'Hara and her unrequited love for Ashley Wilkes and her relationship with and marriage to Rhett Butler, played out against the Civil War–era South. (2) As a teenager the beautiful and willful Scarlet O'Hara falls in love with neighboring plantation owner Ashley Wilkes and maintains her unrequited love for Ashley through his marriage to Melanie Hampton and her marriages to Melanie's brother Charles, to Frank Kennedy, and finally to Rhett Butler. (3) The relationship between Rhett Butler and Scarlett O'Hara begins before the Civil War when they meet at Ashley's plantation; continues through her two earlier marriages, the fall and burning of Atlanta by Sherman's Union soldiers, the defeat and reconstruction of the South; and finally culminates in their marriage, the birth and death of their only child Bonnie, and the eventual disintegration of the marriage. (4) The relationships

WRITING A SUMMARY
Choose a textbook chapter you've just read or something you need to summarize for a class and write a five-sentence summary paragraph.

of the main characters are played out against the changes brought by the Civil War, beginning with the South's secession from the Union, the bloody years of battle, and finally the Reconstruction. **(5)** Mitchell's novel not only is the story of Scarlett O'Hara and her relationships but is a vivid recounting of the events of the Civil War and how they affected and changed the South forever.

V. WRITING A RESEARCH PAPER

Doing Some Groundwork

1. **Identify the basic requirements for the paper**. These might include the following:
   a. Topic restrictions, if any
   b. Paper length
   c. Required number of sources
   d. Types of sources required
   e. Format requirements
   f. Material to be turned in with the paper
   g. Due date, or due dates if you have to turn in parts before the final paper
2. **Prepare a project breakdown**. This should include due dates to help pace yourself through this type of lengthy assignment.

DOING THE GROUNDWORK

If you have a report or a research paper to write for one of your classes, collect the necessary information about the assignment and plan how and when you'll work on the project.

3. **Choose your topic carefully**. The prior section on topic choice gives an effective way to brainstorm and then narrow possible topics. Alternatively, you can develop several limited topics using broader ones. If necessary read an encyclopedia article on the topics to get some basic ideas and information. Once you have two or three possible topics, check the library to make sure enough reference materials are available.

Preparing a Working Bibliography

1. **Put together your working bibliography**. A working bibliography is a list of potential sources that contains four times the actual number of final sources needed for the paper. You'll probably have to make several trips to the library. On 3 × 5 notecards, in standard bibliographical format, collect a file of all possible sources. The library project beginning on page 195 explains how to locate information in a library.

Note: A research time-saver is to locate one or more published bibliographies and scan these for potential sources for your paper. Quick, efficient ways to locate bibliographies are given in the library project. Normally, one or two bibliographies are sufficient to gather the required number of sources.

Taking Reading Notes

1. **Schedule some reading time**. These work sessions should be spaced over several weeks. Begin with the most general sources or with the ones most likely to provide details to support your thesis. An encyclopedia article is often a good first choice. Many such articles also list additional reference sources.

2. **Take notes on the reading material**. Use an organized method. Consult a research manual, such as Coyle's *Research Methods*, for possible note formats. Make sure that you code each card as to its source.

EXERCISE A.9

PREPARING A WORKING BIBLIOGRAPHY

If you have a report or a research paper to write for one of your classes, prepare a working bibliography using 3 × 5 notecards.

Making an Outline

1. **Use notecards to create an outline of your paper**. If you have taken one idea note per card, it is easy and fast to sort the notecards into several piles of subject stacks. The outline can be formed from these piles of notecards.

Writing the Paper

1. **Write a rough draft**. If possible, write on a word processor. Also, try to space out your writing sessions, doing one or two sections of the outline at one work session. Use your card codes to indicate the sources of quotes and paraphrases. Later, you can use one work session to focus on writing your footnotes and bibliography.

EXERCISE A.10

TAKING RESEARCH NOTES

Consult several books or chapters on how to write a research paper to find several ways of taking research notes. If you do this with a group, share your results. If you have a report or a research paper to write for one of your classes, use one of the methods you discovered for taking notes and try it out to see how it works for you. You may choose to test two note-taking methods.

EXERCISE A.11

CREATING AN OUTLINE

If you have a report or a research paper to write for one of your classes, create your detailed outline by sorting your notecards. Then, write out your working outline, using either a traditional left-brained outline format or the right-brained spidergram.

2. **Leave the rough draft for a time**. Then, reread it, checking for logic, necessary support and paragraph development, and grammatical and spelling errors. Edit and correct as needed.

3. **Mark the footnote/endnote numbers**. As you do this, list the source and page number on a separate page. Doing this details-oriented task at one time lets you concentrate fully on it.

4. **Type the endnote pages, bibliography page, coversheet, and so on**. If you have written the sources on individual 3 × 5 notecards in standard bibliographical form, all you need to do is alphabetize and type them.

5. **Proofread the paper before submitting**. A good way to proofread is to read the paper backwards: start with the last word of the paper and read each word from the end of the paper to the first word. Often, undetected errors will be found using this method. Even if you have grammar and spelling check programs on your computer, read the paper yourself. Grammar and spelling check programs do not capture all errors.

6. **Always make and keep a photo or computer copy of the paper before turning it in**.

VI. USING THE ACADEMIC LIBRARY

The library project that follows will teach you how your college library works and how to find information for a research paper. The project is set up so that it can be a class assignment. Your instructor may choose to have you do the entire project or one part at a time. This project is designed to be self-explanatory. You will be able to complete the project by *reading* the textual information between questions and then *searching* for the library location of the item, and *thinking* to find the answers to the questions.

Library research requires thinking and detective work. Items that can be completed using the textbook, lecture notes, information provided in the research section of this chapter, or information typically provided by libraries are preceded by an asterisk. Check with your college library's information or reference desk to find out what type of materials describing your college library are available. If you are doing this as a class assignment, concentrate on completing the nonasterisked items while you are in the library. Otherwise, use the various sections to help you find the reference materials you need.

Part I: Using Bibliographic and Library Tools

Goal of Part I These items are designed to teach you about the research process, to show you how to use various library tools, and to give you information about your college library.

The research process At the beginning of the research process, in one or two work sessions, compile four times the number of final sources you expect to use in your paper. This is not as difficult as it sounds if you use the shortcuts to potential reference sources as outlined in this library project. In actual research you would probably need to locate only one or two of these, but for this project familiarize yourself with all these reference sources:

- Encyclopedias, including any online encyclopedias your college library has in its computer system
- Books that contain only sources—called bibliographies— or books that contain bibliographies
- Bibliographic indexes
- Library guides to a specific subject, if your library provides these

*1. Define a bibliography.

　　_____

　　_____

*2. Define a bibliography as used in a research paper.

　　_____

　　_____

*3. Define a working bibliography as used in the preparation of a research paper.

　　_____

　　_____

Reference stacks Some libraries place often-used reference books together. Check to see if your library does this. If so, complete this section.

4. While browsing in the reference stacks, select a book whose title surprises you (you are surprised to find that such a book was published) but that you think contains useful information:
   Title _____ Call # _____
5. While browsing in the reference stacks, select any book that you would like to write or be referenced in someday:
   Title _____ Call # _____

Almanacs Almanacs are very helpful for locating a number of facts quickly.

6. Locate an almanac in your library and complete the following:

Title/date _____ Call # _____

7. List three kinds of information found in the almanac:

a. _____

b. _____

c. _____

Biographical information Sometimes you need information about someone's life. Locate where your library places biographical reference material. Check to see if your library has the *Biography and Genealogy Master Index (BGMI)*. The *BGMI* is a tremendous time-saver because it indexes more than 400 biographical sources including the *Biography Index* and *Current Biography*. Usually, a number of biographical sources are listed by code (explanations for the code are given in the front of the book). If your library contains the *BGMI*, look up the name of a famous historical person and complete the following:

8. Information about this person can be found in the following (list the codes and their meanings):

a. _____

b. _____

c. _____

9. If you wanted to find information on this person, what would you do now? (thinking question) _____

_____

_____

Special services Libraries typically offer a number of special services, including those listed below.

* 10. Check to see if your library offers these services, and state the location and purpose of each service:

a. Copy services _____

_____

b. Microforms _____

_____

c. Government documents _____

_____

d. Interlibrary loan _____

_____

e. Computer searches _____

_____

f. Reserve book services _____

_____

* 11. List any other special services your library offers. Give their names, locations, and a brief statement of the services provided.

a. _____
_____

b. _____
_____

* 12. List the phone number to call to find out the hours your library is open: _____
_____

* 13. Does your college have more than one library? If so, name them:

a. _____ c. _____
b. _____ d. _____

* 14. Other than books and magazines, list three types of resources provided by your library:

a. _____
b. _____
c. _____

Part II: Finding Books

Goal of Part II These items are designed to teach you how to locate books in your college library. As directed by your instructor, choose a subject to be used for this project or use a topic you need to research. Fill in a general topic name for your subject below:

_____

Finding subject headings Once you have selected a general topic, you will need to discover the exact name or phrasing used by librarians to file material on that topic. This helps you avoid a very frustrating problem—looking up topics under headings that don't exist.

The *Library of Congress Subject Headings (LCSH)* volumes will tell you what heading(s) your topic is filed under in the library. The *LCSH* is an important tool for broadening or narrowing a paper topic and for determining the correct library terminology for topics. Using the *LCSH*, look up your topic to find three related subject headings. You may need to broaden or narrow your topic by following the *LCSH* subdivisions: *BT* for *broader term*, *NT* for *narrower term*, *RT* for *related term*, and *SA* for *see also*.

15. List three subject headings that could be used for your topic here:

a. _____
b. _____
c. _____

Using the library catalog First, you need to determine how your library catalogs books. Two typical methods are the traditional card catalog system and the computerized database. If your library uses a card catalog, you'll find a series of drawers of 3 × 5 cards, one for each book the library owns. Typically, these cards are divided into three sections: author, book title, and subject. In general, you'll use the subject section more than the other two. Look up your topic by subject heading and then copy the bibliographical information provided on the card.

Computer catalogs often consist of a number of different databases providing access to books, journal indexes, newspapers, reference works, career services information, and specialized collection information. Instructions for using the online catalog are usually posted near the terminals. In addition, the computer catalogs are usually available through dial-in access from home computers with modems.

Go to your college library's card or computer catalog. Check instructions for its use.

16. Briefly explain how to use the catalog. If you are using a computer catalog, give the codes and their meaning for accessing the various sections of the catalog.

    _____

    _____

    _____

    _____

17. How many books are listed for your subject? _____

    _____

Continue using the catalog until you come to the bibliographic information for *two* of the books. To do this you will need to look at the full record for the books. This will be given on the 3 × 5 card, but on a computer catalog you may have to request the full record screen.

18. List the bibliographic information for your first book:
    a. Author (last/first name) _____
    b. Title _____
    c. City/publisher/date of pub._____
    d. Call # _____
    e. Is the book checked out? _____ How do you know? _____
19. Now repeat the process for your second book:
    a. Author (last/first name) _____
    b. Title _____
    c. City/publisher/date of pub._____
    d. Call # _____
    e. Is the book checked out? _____ How do you know? _____
*20. How do you know where books with certain call numbers are shelved? _____

21. On what floor or in what library would you find your first book? _____

22. On what floor or in what library would you find your second book? _____

Let's pretend that the books you need are not on the shelf (do not go look, but assume that you did). If they are not on the shelf, do not panic, but prepare to do some detective work.

* 23. Assume that a book you want is neither checked out nor on the proper shelf. Name at least four places it might be: (thinking question)
  a. _____   c. _____
  b. _____   d. _____

* 24. Assume that the book you want is currently checked out. How can you have it saved for your use? What do you do? Where do you go to do it?

  _____

  _____

* 25. Where is the circulation service and what does it do?

  _____

  _____

* 26. How do you check out a book in your library?

  _____

  _____

* 27. For how long can an undergraduate check out a book?

  _____

  _____

* 28. What is the penalty if the book is not returned on time?

  _____

  _____

* 29. Summarize how you find books in your college library:
  a. _____
  b. _____
  c. _____
  d. _____
  e. _____

Using prepared bibliographies In your college library catalog, find a book that is strictly a bibliography. Usually, such works will have the word *bibliography* as part of the title.

30. List the bibliography information:
  a. Author _____
  b. Title _____   Call # _____

Now, locate the bibliography and browse through it.

31. List two sources (books or journal articles) from the bibliography that you could use to find information on your topic. Fill in all appropriate blanks:
   a. Author (last/first name) _____
   b. Title _____
   c. City/publisher/date/pages _____
32. Now repeat the process for your second source:
   a. Author (last/first name) _____
   b. Title _____
   c. City/publisher/date/pages _____

Using the bibliographic index Using this reference (if your library owns it), find a book *or* a periodical article on your topic. All sources listed in this type of index contain a bibliography, so you can use sources found here to locate other sources on your topic.

33. For the book or journal on your topic, list the following:
   a. Author (last/first name) _____
   b. Title of book or journal _____
   c. Title of article (if journal) _____
   d. Pages (if listed)/publication date _____

Part III: Finding Journal/Serial/Periodical/ Magazine/Newspaper Articles

Goal of Part III These questions are designed to teach you how to locate journal/serial/periodical/magazine/annual/newspaper articles as a part of library research. For the purposes of most undergraduates, journals, serials, magazines, annuals, periodicals, and newspapers are similar types of publications and can be accessed in the same way.

The research process Finding articles is a four-part process:

* 1. Select an index (electronic via computer, CD-ROM, or paper) that contains articles about your topic.
* 2. In your selected index find the name of an article that you could use, and interpret the information given to determine in which magazine or journal the article is published (this is called a *citation*).
* 3. Use the list of library-owned magazines (often called a Periodicals or Public Serials List (PSL) to see if your library has the magazine you need.
* 4. Find the article.

The following questions will incorporate each of these steps, but first read any information your library provides on how to find articles in journals and magazines.

About indexes Most college libraries contain many indexes, most of which are subject indexes. A *general index*, such as the *Readers' Guide to Periodical Literature*, covers articles on general and popular topics. A *subject index* includes professional journal articles from a specific subject area. For example, the *Social Science Index* covers areas such as sociology, psychology, and political science.

34. Use the *Readers' Guide to Periodical Literature* to locate a magazine article on or related to your topic:
    a. Author (last/first name) _____
    b. Title of magazine article _____
    c. Title of magazine _____
    d. Vol. #/month, year of pub./pages _____

Note: Check the front for the complete title of magazine abbreviations.

Subject indexes Find out where your library shelves the *subject indexes*. Using an appropriate subject index, find a second article on your topic. If you are not sure what subject index to use, ask your instructor or a reference librarian.

35. For your subject index, list the following:
    a. Title _____
    b. Call # _____ Location _____
36. Now look up a second article on your subject:
    a. Author (last/first name) _____
    b. Title of journal article _____
    c. Title of journal _____
    d. Vol. #/month, year of pub./pages _____

Now browse through some other subject indexes. Recall that subject indexes list professional journals in one specific field such as education, humanities, or business. Find two different indexes that you could use for research in your major and/or for this project.

Note: In completing items 37 and 38, you do *not* have to stick to your chosen subject.

37. a. Title of subject index _____
    b. Call # _____ Table location # _____
    c. List two journals indexed in this subject index (or two types of information found in it):

    _____

    _____

38. a. Title of subject index _____
    b. Call # _____ Table location # _____

c. List two journals indexed in this subject index (or two types of information found in it):

_____

_____

If your library also indexes magazines in a computer database, go back to the computer catalog. This time you are going to find a journal article using the computer. From the databases screen, choose one of the available journal indexes shown. From this index, find a third article on or related to your subject.

39. Name of journal index _____
40. Topics and/or journals covered _____
41. Now list the following for your chosen article:
    a. Author (last/first name) _____
    b. Title of journal article _____
    c. Title of journal _____
    d. Vol. #/month, year of pub./pages _____

Go to the newspaper indexes and check one for an article on or related to your topic and answer the following:

42. a. Name of index _____
    b. Year of index _____ Call # _____
    c. Title of newspaper _____
    d. Title of article (shortened since most newspaper indexes give summaries of the article, not titles)

    _____

    e. Date of article _____ Pages _____

Periodical serials list (PSL) Using the PSL or the reference source your library uses to list magazines it owns, answer these questions:

43. a. Title of journal/magazine in item 34 _____
    b. Call # _____ Vols. and years library has

    _____

    c. Any additional information listed _____
44. a. Title of journal/magazine in item 36 or 41 _____
    b. Call # _____ Vols. and years library has

    _____

    c. Any additional information listed _____
45. a. Title of newspaper in item 42 _____
    b. Call # _____ Vols. and years library has

    _____

    c. Any additional information listed _____

Finding the journal

* 46. a. Where does the library keep bound issues of journals (over one year old)?

_____

b. How are they shelved? _____

* 47. Where does the library keep unbound journals (periodicals)?

Name of location _____ Library level _____

Now actually locate one of the journals you listed in previous items. Yes, you may have to try more than one of your sources before you find the article, and yes, you must leave the main floor of the library to do this.

48. a. Name of journal found _____
    b. Item # _____
49. Where found? _____

Summing it up

* 50. List the steps in the process of finding journals in your library:

a. _____
b. _____
c. _____
d. _____
e. _____
f. _____
g. _____

* 51. What are three sources you can use to find journal articles in your library? How do you use each one? (_Hint:_ You used each for this project.)

a. _____
_____

b. _____
_____

c. _____
_____

* 52. If you still have any questions about how to use the library, list them here:

a. _____
_____

b. _____
_____

c. _____
_____

Notes

[1]From *John Donne's Poetry*, A. L. Clements, ed. (New York: Norton, 1966).

[2]Suggestions for explicating a poem based on K. B. Valentine and D. E. Valentine, *Interlocking Pieces: Twenty Questions for Understanding Literature*, 2nd ed. (Dubuque, Iowa: Kendall/Hunt, 1980).

[3]Suggested by John D. Mildrew.

[4]Adapted from Bobby J. Woodruff, *Terms, Tables, and Skills for the Physical Sciences* (Morristown, N.J.: Silver Burdett Company, 1966), and from information provided by John D. Mildrew, chairman of the Math-Science Department at South Mountain Community College, Phoenix, Arizona.

Appendix B

College Services and Procedures

This appendix lists typical college services, offices, and helping resources and gives you blanks in which to record key information. Note that no one school will offer all of these services, and no one student will use all of them. However, you can use these lists to learn about services you might need and about your college in general. *Do not try to complete all the lists.* Some resources you will use; some you will find helpful next year or the year after; some you won't ever need. Consider making a copy of these pages to keep in your notebook or recording information on notecards, one per resource. Add information as you need it or learn it. You may find it useful to work with a group to collect information and share it.

Overview of the List Groups

I. **Becoming a Student:** Admission or Transfer Procedures; Orientation; Advisement; Registration; Fees and Tuition; and Rearranging the Class Schedule

II. **Basic Necessities of Life:** Housing; Food; Restaurants; Groceries; Drugstore; Hair Care; Laundromat.

III. **Health and Physical Fitness:** Medical and Dental Services; Wellness and Psychological/Counseling Services; Exercise Facilities

IV. **Parking and Transportation:** Parking on Campus; Bicycle Repair; Wheelchair Repair; Travel Agency

V. **Money:** Discounts; Scholarship Office; Employment; Financial Aid

VI. **Getting a Life:** "In" Places to Go; State and College Drinking and Drug Laws and Regulations; Clubs and Organizations; Sports

VII. **Being a Student:** Learning and Tutoring Centers; Study Abroad Services; Study Skills Center; Testing Services; Bookstores; Computer Center; Photocopying

VIII. **Student Services:** Career Services/Placement Office; Dean of Students; Legal Services; Minority Student Services; Student Newspaper; Student Government; Student Services/ Student Affairs; Disabled Student Services; International Student Services; Returning/Adult Student Services/ Veterans Services

I. BECOMING A STUDENT

Admission or Transfer Procedures

Admissions office _____

Location _____ Phone _____

Hours _____ Contact person _____

Application procedures _____

Application deadlines _____

Required documents _____

Orientation

Orientation office _____

Location _____ Phone _____

Hours _____ Contact person _____

Early orientation dates _____

Summer orientation dates _____

Presemester orientation dates _____

Orientation fees (if any) _____

Advisement

Colleges often have a number of different types of advisors. You may find it helpful to use several. Determine which types of advisors your school has and how you obtain advising services.

Is advising mandatory? _____ For whom? _____

General advising _____

Location _____ Phone _____

Hours _____ Contact person _____

College advisors _____

Location _____ Phone _____

Hours _____ Contact person _____

Major advisors _____

Location _____ Phone _____

Hours _____ Contact person _____

Career advisors _____

Location _____ Phone _____

Hours _____ Contact person _____

Advisors for professional degrees

Dentistry _____

Law _____

Medicine _____

Physical therapy _____

Other _____

Registration

Registration site(s) _____

Location _____ Phone _____

Hours _____ Contact person _____

Preregistration dates _____

Preregistration process _____

_____

Regular registration dates _____

Regular registration process _____

_____

Late registration dates _____

Late registration process _____

_____

Late penalty _____

Fees and Tuition

Fees per credit hour _____

Number of credit hours needed to be considered a full-time student _____

Tuition for full-time students _____

Payment process _____

Late registration fees _____

Rearranging the Class Schedule

Dates for dropping or adding classes _____

Drop/add process _____

_____

Drop/add penalty (if any) _____

Dates for adding classes _____

Dates for withdrawing from individual classes _____

Dates for withdrawing from school _____

Withdrawal penalties _____

Tuition refund policies after withdrawal _____

II. BASIC NECESSITIES OF LIFE

On-campus housing office _____

Location _____ Phone _____

Hours _____ Contact person _____

Types available _____

Costs _____

Application process _____

_____

Must you sign a contract? _____

General provisions of contract _____

Penalties for not fulfilling the contract _____

Off-campus housing office _____

Location _____ Phone _____

Hours _____ Contact person _____

Other sources of information _____

_____

School regulations (if any) _____

_____

On-campus food service _____

Location _____ Phone _____

Hours _____ Contact person _____

Service system (e.g., meal ticket, pay per meal) _____

Names and locations of other on-campus sources of food _____

_____

Inexpensive off-campus restaurant _____

Location _____ Phone _____

Medium-priced off-campus restaurant _____

Location _____ Phone _____

Expensive off-campus restaurant _____

Location _____ Phone _____

On-campus grocery _____

Location _____ Phone _____

Hours _____

Off-campus grocery _____

Location _____ Phone _____

Hours _____

On-campus drugstore _____

Location _____ Phone _____

Hours _____ Contact person _____

Off-campus drugstore _____

Location _____ Phone _____

Hours _____ Contact person _____

On-campus barber/beauty salon _____

Location _____ Phone _____

Hours _____ Contact person _____

Off-campus barber/beauty salon _____

Location _____ Phone _____

Hours _____ Contact person _____

On-campus laundromat _____

Location _____ Phone _____

Hours _____

Off-campus laundromat _____

Location _____ Phone _____

Hours _____

III. HEALTH AND PHYSICAL FITNESS

Student health insurance (if any) _____

Coverage offered _____

Application process _____

Cost _____

On-campus medical services _____

Location _____ Phone _____

Hours _____ Contact person _____

Requirements for using _____

_____

Summary of services provided _____

_____

Off-campus medical services _____

Location _____ Phone _____

Hours _____ Contact person _____

On-campus dental services _____

Location _____ Phone _____

Hours _____ Contact person _____

Requirements for using _____

_____

Summary of services provided _____

_____

Off-campus dental services _____

Location _____ Phone _____

Hours _____ Contact person _____

On-campus counseling/psychological services _____

Location _____ Phone _____

Hours _____ Contact person _____

Summary of services provided _____

_____

Off-campus counseling/psychological services _____

Location _____ Phone _____

Hours _____ Contact person _____

Other on-campus wellness services _____

Location _____ Phone _____

Hours _____ Contact person _____

Requirements for using _____

_____

Summary of services provided _____

_____

Other off-campus wellness services _____

Location _____ Phone _____

Hours _____ Contact person _____

On-campus exercise facilities _____

Location _____ Phone _____

Hours _____ Contact person _____

Cost (if any) _____

Off-campus exercise facilities _____

Location _____ Phone _____

Hours _____ Contact person _____

Cost _____

IV. PARKING AND TRANSPORTATION

Driving and parking on campus

Forms of transportation permitted on campus _____

_____

General parking regulations _____

_____

Decal/permit required? _____

Acquisition process _____

Documents needed _____

_____

Cost of a decal/permit _____

Other forms of transportation for getting to school _____

_____

Transportation information sources _____

On-campus bicycle repair service _____

Location _____ Phone _____

Hours _____ Contact person _____

On-campus wheelchair repair _____

Location _____ Phone _____

Hours _____ Contact person _____

On-campus travel agency _____

Location _____ Phone _____

Hours _____ Contact person _____

V. MONEY

Student discounts

Entertainment? _____

Computers? _____

Other goods and services? _____

Scholarship Office _____

Location _____ Phone _____

Hours _____ Contact person _____

Employment, on-campus _____

Location _____ Phone _____

Hours _____ Contact person _____

Employment, off-campus _____

Location _____ Phone _____

Hours _____ Contact person _____

Financial aid office _____

Location _____ Phone _____

Hours _____ Contact person _____

VI. GETTING A LIFE

"In" places to go _____

Location _____ Phone _____

Alcohol

Drinking age _____

Summary of state drinking laws _____

_____

Penalties _____

Summary of college drinking regulations _____

_____

Penalties _____

Drugs

Summary of state drug laws _____

_____

Penalties _____

Summary of college drug regulations _____

_____

Penalties _____

Clubs and Organizations

Club/organization of interest to you _____

Location _____ Phone _____

Hours _____ Contact person _____

Club/organization of interest to you _____

Location _____ Phone _____

Hours _____ Contact person _____

Club/organization of interest to you _____

Location _____ Phone _____

Hours _____ Contact person _____

Club/organization of interest to you _____

Location _____ Phone _____

Hours _____ Contact person _____

Fraternity/sorority, social _____

Location _____ Phone _____

Hours _____ Contact person _____

Fraternity/sorority, honorary _____

Location _____ Phone _____

Hours _____ Contact person _____

Fraternity/sorority, professional _____

Location _____ Phone _____

Hours _____ Contact person _____

Sports, intramural _____

Location _____ Phone _____

Hours _____ Contact person _____

Sports, tickets _____

Location _____ Phone _____

Hours _____ Contact person _____

VII. BEING A STUDENT

Learning center _____

Location _____ Phone _____

Hours _____ Contact person _____

Math tutoring/learning center _____

Location _____ Phone _____

Hours _____ Contact person _____

Study abroad services _____

Location _____ Phone _____

Hours _____ Contact person _____

Study skills center _____

Location _____ Phone _____

Hours _____ Contact person _____

Testing services _____

Location _____ Phone _____

Hours _____ Contact person _____

Tutoring services _____

Location _____ Phone _____

Hours _____ Contact person _____

Writing center _____

Location _____ Phone _____

Hours _____ Contact person _____

On-campus bookstore _____

Location _____ Phone _____

Hours _____ Contact person _____

Off-campus bookstore _____

Location _____ Phone _____

Hours _____ Contact person _____

Computer center _____

Location _____ Phone _____

Hours _____ Contact person _____

On-campus photocopying _____

Location _____ Phone _____

Hours _____ Contact person _____

VIII. STUDENT SERVICES

General Services

Career Services/Placement Office _____

Location _____ Phone _____

Hours _____ Contact person _____

Dean of Students _____

Location _____ Phone _____

Hours _____ Contact person _____

Legal Services _____

Location _____ Phone _____

Hours _____ Contact person _____

Minority student services _____

Location _____ Phone _____

Hours _____ Contact person _____

Newspaper, student _____

Location _____ Phone _____

Hours _____ Contact person _____

Student government _____

Location _____ Phone _____

Hours _____ Contact person _____

Student services/ student affairs _____

Location _____ Phone _____

Hours _____ Contact person _____

Specific Student Population Services

Disabled student services _____

Location _____ Phone _____

Hours _____ Contact person _____

International student services _____

Location _____ Phone _____

Hours _____ Contact person _____

Returning/adult student services _____

Location _____ Phone _____

Hours _____ Contact person _____

Veterans services _____

Location _____ Phone _____

Hours _____ Contact person _____

Index

Grammar, 158
Grinder, John, 1
Group exams, 131
Group study, 131

H

Hanau, Laia, 76, 85
Highlighting text, 98–100
History, 64
Homework weekly planner, 47
Housing, 208

I

Idea clusters, 75, 79
Identical meanings, 152
Immediate review, 100
Independent learner, 177
Indexes, 201
Informal speaking style assessment, 24
Information patterns, 56–67
Information processes, 2
Information sorter, 58
Instructor's expectations, 70
Insurance, 8
Inter-library loan, 196
Intermediate review, 100–101
International student services, 216

J

Joke answers, 153
Journal index, 200
Journal, 200, 203

K

Kinesthetic, 1–3
Kolb, David 1, 5, 20

L

Laboratory report, 179, 189
Lakein, Alan, 55
Learning and Study Strategies Inventory (LASSI), 21
Learning Center, 214
Learning patterns, 2
Learning style assessments, 21, 26
Learning style inventory, 20
Learning style, 2, 18–28
Lecture notes, 68–85
Left-brain note-taking, 78, 81
Left-brain test taking, 124

Left-brained, 1–4, 24
Legal services, 215
Length, 155
Letter of complaint, 179,
Levy, Jerre, 1
Library catalog, 197
Library of Congress Subject Headings, 197
Library, 194
Lifelong learning, 177
Lists, simple, 59
Literature, 65
Living at home, 10
Living away from home, 10
Loci-based memory devices, 114, 118

M

Magazine, 200
Main idea of the paragraph, 93
Making notes on or in the chapter, 98–100
Managing time, 30–55
Marking, 98–100
Master schedule, 13, 41–44
Matching tests, 146–147
Math, 65–66
Memory devices, 109–119
Memory, 106–119
Myers-Briggs Type Inventory, 20
Middle value, 156
Minority student services, 215
Mnemonics, 112
    for notetaking, 76
Modified outline notetaking, 78, 81
Money, 212
Multiple choice, 144–146

N

Narrative, 180
Nest, 10
Neuro-linguistic programming, 1
Newspaper index, 200
Newspaper, 200, 215
Newspaper, student, 215
NLP, 2
Non-answers, 154
Non-verbal communication, 71
Note-taking guidelines, 71
Note-taking mnemonic, 76
Note-taking, 68–85
Number-rhyme auditory system, 115–116
Number-shape visual system, 117

O

Objective evaluation, 186
Objective tests, 136–163
Odd or extreme choices, 153
Opposite ideas, 155
Organic study method, 89
Orientation, 206
Ostrander, S., 119
Outline, 182, 193
Overview the text, 89, 90

P

Paperwork, college, 9
Parking, 9, 211
Pattern answers, 158
Perfectionists, 53
Periodical index, 200
Periodical, 200
Periodicals or Public Serials List (PSL), 202
Personal learning style summary, 27
Personalizing the text, 88–89
Pre-register, 8
Preview, the chapter, 89, 91
Prime external time (PET), 50
Prime internal time (PIT), 50
Principles, memory, 108
Process, 181
Procrastination, 52–54
Project organizer, 45–46, 48–49,
Psychological/counseling services, 210

Q

Quickplan outlines, 172–174

R

Rate of study, 38
Re-entry students, 32, 216
Reaction, 187
Reader's Guide to Periodical Literature, 201
Reading college textbooks, 86–105
Reading speed, 102–104
Receipts and records, 9, 16
Receipts for fee payments, 9
Reference stacks, 195
Registration, 207
Registration
    classes, 8
    signatures, 8
Relation, 170
Relaxation techniques, 135

Relaxing breathing, 134
Relaxing visualizing, 134
Repetition, 156
Research notes, 193
Research paper, 180, 192
Reserve book services, 196
Residence life, 10
Resume, 180
Review, 50, 100–102
Rewards, 52, 55, 183
Rhymes, 112, 155
Right-brain note-taking, 82
Right-brain test taking, 125
Right-brained, 1–4, 24,
Roommate, 10
Rough draft, 182, 194

S

Scholarship, 8
Science, 66
Semester overview or plan, 41
Sentence completion questions,
    147–149
Sequential lists, 60
Serial Index, 200
Serial, 200
Similar or confusing terms or
    definitions, 127
Similar phrases, 155
Simple list, 59
Single-session study planner, 52
Slanting, 180
Speaking assignments, 181, 183,
    190
Speed and reading 102–104
Sperry, Roger, 1
Spidergram, 82–84, 184

Split pairs, 156
Split-brain research, 1
Spoilers, 144
Starting smart, 6–17
Statement pie, 76
Study abroad, services, 214
Study environment, 28
Study group, 131
Study place, 10–11
Study plan, 128
Studying for tests, 120–135
Subject headings, 197
Subject index, 210
Subject study tips, 62–66
Summary, 180, 186, 191
Syllabus 12, 16

T

Taking objective tests, 136–163
Test anxiety, 133
Test performance, 149
Test questions, predicting, 124
Test strategies, 122, 128, 138
Test taking, left-brain, 124
Test taking, right-brain, 125
Testing services, 214
Tests,
    application, 73
    essay, 73, 164–176
    objective, 72, 136–163
    studying for, 120–135
    subjective, 73, 164
Textbook patterns, 89
Textbooks
    overview, 16
    purchase, 89
Theme, 180

Thesis statement, 182
Time circles, 34–35
Time logs, 34, 36
Time management, 30–55
Time management principles, 39, 48
Time planning, 12
Topic choice, 183–185, 192
Topic narrowing, 181–183
Transfer procedures, 206
Transfer students, 206
True-false techniques, 142, 154
Tuition, 207
Tutoring centers, 214

U

Umbrella answers, 157

V

Veterans services, 216
Visual, 1, 2
Visualizing relaxing, 134
Vocabulary development, 104–105
Vocabulary, 157

W

Weekly schedules, 45, 47, 129
Weekly study hours, estimation of,
    40, 129
Wheelchair repair, 212
Whole-brain approach to time, 37,
    42
Working bibliography, 192
Writing assignments, 179–183
Writing center, 214
Writing essay exams, 164–176